Table of Contents

Curriculum Map

Week 1	Week 2	Week 3	Week 4	Week 5	Week 6
Introduction to STEAM and Design Thinking	Science and Technology	Engineering and Math	Arts and Creativity	Computer Science and Data Science	Culminating Project
Introduction to STEAM concepts and careers	Introduction to basic scientific concepts (e.g. physics, chemistry, biology)	Introduction to different engineering fields (e.g. civil, mechanical, aerospace)	Introduction to different forms of art (e.g. drawing, painting, sculpture, music)	Introduction to computer science concepts (e.g. programming, web development)	Students work in teams to identify a real-world problem and develop a solution using the skills and knowledge they have acquired throughout the camp
Introduction to the design thinking process	Exploration of different types of technology (e.g. coding, robotics, electronics)	Math activities and games to reinforce concepts (e.g. geometry, algebra, statistics)	Exploration of how STEAM and creativity intersect	Introduction to data science concepts (e.g. data analysis, visualization)	Final presentations to showcase their projects and solutions to a panel of judges or the larger community
Design challenge: students work in teams to identify a real-world problem and develop a solution using design thinking principles	Hands-on activities: students build and program robots, create circuits, and conduct science experiments	Design challenge: students work in teams to design and build a structure using engineering principles	Creative project: students work in teams to create a multimedia presentation or performance based on a STEAM-related theme	Hands-on activities: students create websites, write code, and analyze data	

The curriculum is designed to allow for the integration of guest speakers from different STEAM fields, as well as field trips to local museums, labs, or companies. The curriculum will be flexible to allow for adjustments based on student interests and progress. Additionally, students will have the opportunity to engage in career exploration and college readiness activities to better prepare them for their future goals.

Curriculum Summary

The STEAM Camp is a dynamic and immersive program designed to introduce students to the exciting world of Science, Technology, Engineering, Arts, and Mathematics (STEAM). Over the course of six weeks, students will engage in hands-on activities, collaborative projects, and design challenges to foster creativity, critical thinking, and problem-solving skills. This comprehensive program covers a wide range of STEAM disciplines and offers a well-rounded educational experience.

Week 1 focuses on building a solid foundation by introducing students to the fundamental concepts of STEAM and Design Thinking. Participants will explore various STEAM careers and gain an understanding of the design thinking process, preparing them for the challenges ahead.

In Week 2, students dive into the captivating realms of Science and Technology. They will delve into core scientific concepts such as physics, chemistry, and biology, while simultaneously exploring different technologies such as coding, robotics, and electronics. Through hands-on activities, students will have the opportunity to build and program robots, create circuits, and conduct science experiments.

Week 3 shifts the focus to Engineering and Math. Students will be introduced to different engineering fields, including civil, mechanical, and aerospace engineering. Additionally, they will engage in math activities and games that reinforce essential concepts like geometry, algebra, and statistics. The highlight of this week is a design challenge where students work collaboratively to design and construct a structure using engineering principles.

Week 4 emphasizes the importance of Arts and Creativity in the STEAM field. Participants will explore various forms of art, such as drawing, painting, sculpture, and music. They will also investigate how creativity intersects with STEAM, inspiring innovative thinking. In teams, students will embark on a creative project, culminating in a multimedia presentation or performance centered around a STEAM-related theme.

Curriculum Summary

Week 5 focuses on Computer Science and Data Science, two rapidly evolving disciplines. Students will learn programming and web development concepts in computer science and gain an understanding of data analysis and visualization in data science. Engaging in hands-on activities, they will have the opportunity to create websites, write code, and analyze data.

Finally, Week 6 serves as the culmination of the camp. Students will utilize the skills and knowledge they have acquired throughout the program to identify a real-world problem. Working in teams, they will employ the principles of STEAM and Design Thinking to develop a viable solution. The program concludes with final presentations, where students showcase their projects and solutions to a panel of judges or the larger community.

The STEAM Camp provides an enriching and comprehensive educational experience, nurturing students' curiosity, fostering their creativity, and equipping them with valuable skills for the future. By embracing the interdisciplinary nature of STEAM, this program empowers students to become well-rounded innovators, ready to tackle real-world challenges with confidence.

Week 1

Introduction to STEAM and Design Thinking

Introduction to STEAM Concepts and Careers

Objective: Introduce students to the basic concepts of STEAM (Science, Technology, Engineering, Arts, and Mathematics) and explore various career opportunities in these fields.

Materials:

- Whiteboard or chart paper
- Markers or chalk
- Handouts with STEAM career examples

Procedure:

1. Warm-up Activity (10 minutes):
   - Ask students to brainstorm examples of science, technology, engineering, arts, and mathematics in their daily lives.
   - Write their responses on the whiteboard or chart paper.
2. Introduction to STEAM (15 minutes):
   - Define STEAM as an interdisciplinary approach that combines different fields to solve problems and create innovative solutions.
   - Explain the importance of STEAM in various industries and how it impacts our lives.
   - Discuss the benefits of pursuing STEAM careers, such as job opportunities, creativity, and critical thinking skills.
3. Exploring STEAM Careers (20 minutes):
   - Distribute handouts with examples of different STEAM careers.
   - Ask students to read the descriptions and discuss the roles, skills, and qualifications required for each career.
   - Facilitate a class discussion by asking students to share their thoughts and questions about the careers.
4. Reflection and Closure (10 minutes):
   - Ask students to reflect on the STEAM careers discussed and identify which ones interest them the most.
   - Encourage students to share their reflections and reasons for their choices.
   - Summarize the key points discussed in the lesson and highlight the importance of STEAM in today's world.

STEAM Careers: Exploring the Exciting Pathways Ahead!

What is STEAM? STEAM stands for Science, Technology, Engineering, Arts, and Mathematics. It's an interdisciplinary approach to learning that combines creativity, critical thinking, and problem-solving skills. STEAM careers offer a world of exciting opportunities where you can explore your passions and make a difference. Let's dive into some fascinating examples of STEAM careers:

- <u>Robotics Engineer:</u> Do you love building and programming robots? As a robotics engineer, you can design and develop innovative robots for various applications, such as space exploration, manufacturing, healthcare, and entertainment.
- <u>App Developer:</u> In a world filled with smartphones and tablets, app developers play a crucial role. They create mobile applications for different platforms, such as iOS and Android, making our lives easier and more enjoyable.
- <u>Environmental Scientist:</u> Passionate about protecting our planet? Environmental scientists study the environment, conduct research, and develop solutions to environmental issues like climate change, pollution, and conservation.
- <u>Video Game Designer:</u> Combine your love for art and technology by becoming a video game designer. You can create captivating virtual worlds, design characters, and develop immersive gameplay experiences for gamers worldwide.
- <u>Biomedical Engineer:</u> If you're interested in medicine and engineering, consider a career as a biomedical engineer. These professionals develop and improve medical devices and technologies, such as prosthetics, artificial organs, and imaging systems.
- <u>Architect:</u> Architects blend creativity, mathematics, and engineering principles to design incredible structures. From skyscrapers to sustainable homes, architects shape the physical spaces we live and work in.
- <u>Data Scientist:</u> Data scientists work with vast amounts of data to discover patterns, draw insights, and solve complex problems. They apply mathematics, statistics, and programming skills to extract valuable information.
- <u>Graphic Designer:</u> Graphic designers use their artistic skills and technological expertise to create visually appealing designs for advertisements, logos, websites, and various other mediums.
- <u>Astronomer:</u> Dream of exploring the mysteries of the universe? Astronomers study celestial bodies, conduct research, and make significant discoveries about space, galaxies, and planets.

- <u>Civil Engineer:</u> Civil engineers design and construct infrastructure projects like bridges, roads, buildings, and dams. They play a vital role in shaping the physical environment around us.

Remember, these are just a few examples of the diverse STEAM careers available. Explore your interests, continue learning, and follow your passions to embark on an exciting journey in the world of STEAM!

Resources for Further Exploration:
- National Girls Collaborative Project: <u>www.ngcproject.org</u>
- STEM Careers: <u>www.stemcareers.com</u>
- NASA STEM Engagement: <u>www.nasa.gov/stem</u>

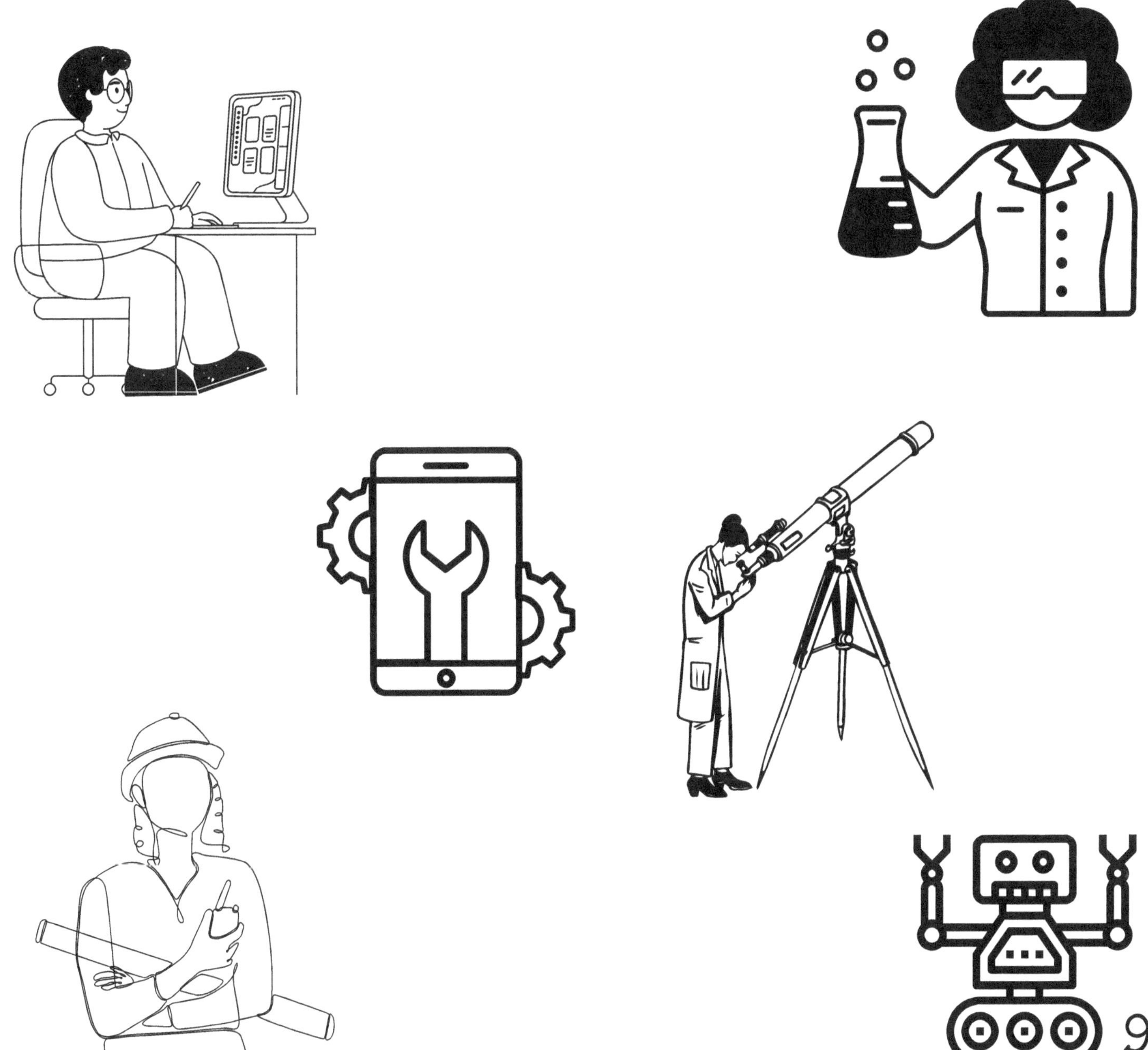

Introduction to the Design Thinking Process

Objective: Introduce students to the design thinking process and its various stages.

Materials:

- Whiteboard or chart paper
- Markers or chalk
- Design thinking process handouts

Procedure:

1. Warm-up Activity (10 minutes):
   - Ask students to think about a real-world problem they would like to solve.
   - Give them a few minutes to write down their ideas individually.
2. Introduction to Design Thinking (15 minutes):
   - Define design thinking as a human-centered problem-solving approach that involves empathy, ideation, prototyping, and testing.
   - Explain the importance of understanding the needs of the users when developing solutions.
   - Discuss examples of successful products or innovations created using design thinking.
3. Design Thinking Process Overview (20 minutes):
   - Display the design thinking process on the whiteboard or chart paper.
   - Break down each stage (Empathize, Define, Ideate, Prototype, Test) and explain its purpose and activities involved.
   - Use examples or case studies to illustrate each stage of the process.
4. Application Activity (15 minutes):
   - Divide students into small groups.
   - Provide each group with a design challenge or problem statement related to a real-world issue.
   - Instruct the groups to brainstorm ideas and sketch a rough solution using the design thinking process.
5. Reflection and Closure (10 minutes):
   - Ask each group to share their design ideas and explain how they applied the design thinking process.
   - Lead a class discussion to reflect on the activity and discuss the benefits and challenges of using design thinking.

Resources for Further Exploration:

- Stanford d.school's "Bootcamp Bootleg" toolkit: dschool.stanford.edu/resources/design-thinking-bootleg
- "Design Thinking for Kids" by David Lee and Emma Trithart
- TED-Ed lesson on "The Five Steps of Design Thinking": ed.ted.com/lessons/the-five-steps-of-design-thinking-ted-ed
- IDEO: www.ideo.com/method-cards
- Design Thinking for Educators: www.designthinkingforeducators.com

Design Thinking: Unleash Your Creative Problem-Solving Superpowers!

What is Design Thinking? Design Thinking is a human-centered approach to problem-solving that encourages creativity, empathy, and innovation. It's a step-by-step process that helps you understand people's needs, brainstorm ideas, and develop practical solutions. Let's dive into the different stages of the Design Thinking process:

- <u>Empathize:</u> Put yourself in the shoes of the people you're designing for. Interview, observe, and empathize with them to gain a deep understanding of their needs, feelings, and challenges. Ask questions like:
  - What problems are they facing?
  - How do they feel about those problems?
  - What are their hopes and aspirations?
- <u>Define:</u> Based on your empathy findings, define the problem you want to solve. Create a clear problem statement that captures the essence of the challenge. For example:
  - How might we create a safer and more enjoyable school environment for students?
- <u>Ideate:</u> Now it's time to generate creative ideas! Encourage wild thinking and come up with as many ideas as possible. Use brainstorming techniques like mind mapping, sketching, or sticky notes. Remember, no idea is too big or too small. Quantity is key at this stage.
- <u>Prototype:</u> Turn your ideas into tangible prototypes. Prototypes can be physical models, drawings, or even role-playing scenarios. The goal is to create something that represents your ideas and can be tested and improved upon.
- <u>Test:</u> Test your prototypes with the people you're designing for. Gather feedback, observe how they interact with your prototypes, and listen to their thoughts. What works? What needs improvement? Refine your designs based on the feedback you receive.
- <u>Iterate:</u> Based on the test results, make improvements to your prototypes. Refine your ideas, make changes, and go through the design thinking process again. Each iteration brings you closer to an innovative solution.

Design Thinking Tips:

- Embrace curiosity and ask "why" and "what if" questions.
- Work collaboratively and listen to different perspectives.
- Embrace failure as a stepping stone to success.
- Be open-minded and willing to iterate and improve.

Design Thinking in Action: Design thinking can be applied to various situations. Here are a few examples:

- Redesigning a school library to make it more inviting and accessible.
- Creating a sustainable packaging solution for a product.
- Developing a user-friendly app for organizing homework and assignments.

Design thinking empowers you to be a problem solver, creative thinker, and empathetic designer. Embrace the process, have fun, and unlock your potential to make a positive impact on the world!

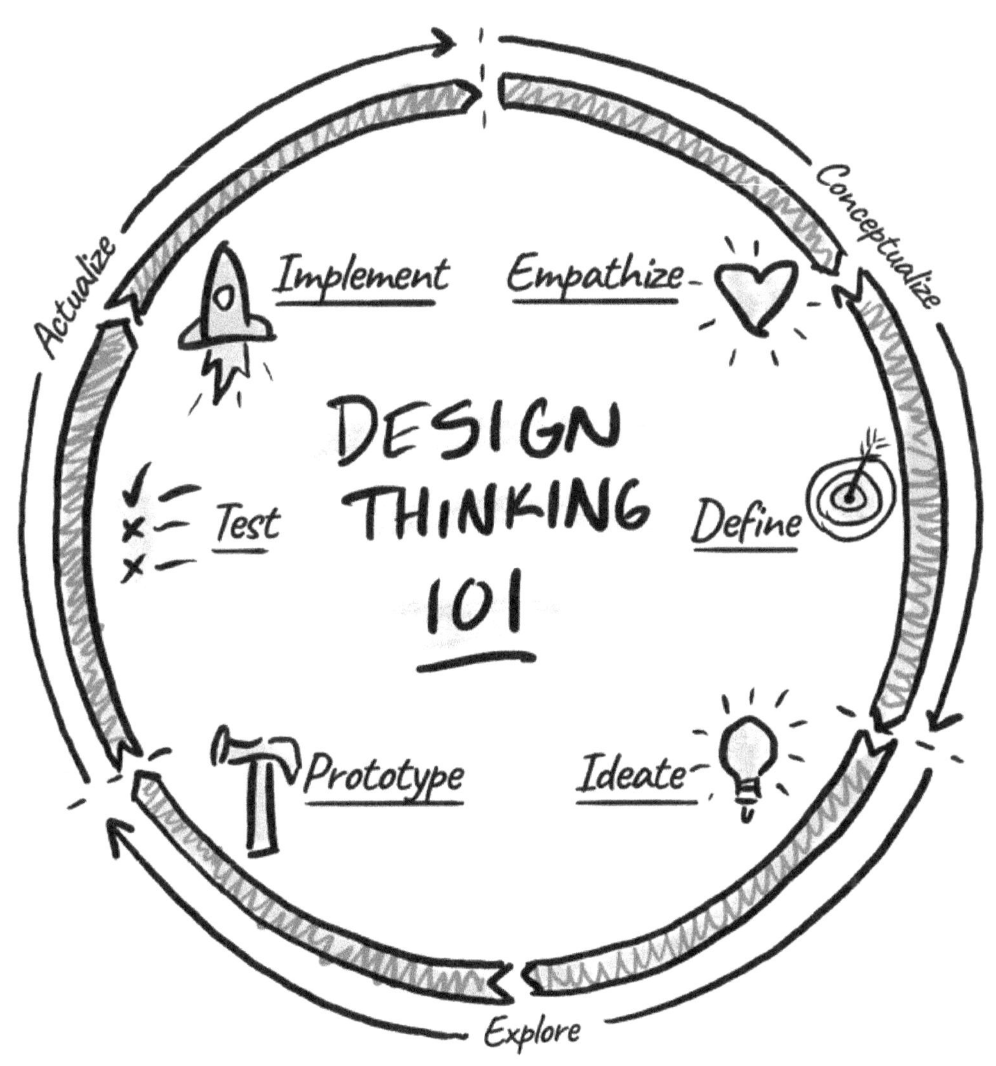

Photo by: (Voltage Control 5 Steps of the Design Thinking Process: A Step-by-Step Guide)

Design Challenge - Identifying a Real-World Problem

Objective: Engage students in a design challenge that requires them to find a solution to the real-world problem given to them.

Materials:
- Whiteboard or chart paper
- Markers, chalk, colored pencils, or other art supplies
- Design challenge handout
- Recyclable or biodegradable materials (cardboard, paper, fabric, etc.)
- Scissors, glue, tape
- Optional: Any other materials you think might be useful for your design (recycled materials, natural elements, etc.)

Procedure: (Day 1 of 2)

1. Introduction (10 minutes):
   - Review the design thinking process briefly, emphasizing the importance of identifying real-world problems.
   - Explain that the students will be working in teams to try to create a solution to the problem provided in the design challenge using design thinking principles.

2. Design Challenge Instructions (15 minutes):
   - Distribute the design challenge handout to each team.
   - Explain the requirements and constraints of the design challenge.
   - Encourage students to think broadly and consider problems that affect their community or the world at large.

3. Team Brainstorming (20 minutes):
   - Instruct the teams to brainstorm potential problems that align with the design challenge.
   - Encourage them to consider different perspectives and discuss the impact of each problem.

4. Planning(15 minutes):
   - Ask each team to work together to make a plan for their prototype.

5. Presentations and Discussion (20 minutes):
   - Give each team an opportunity to present their chosen solution and its definition.
   - Facilitate a class discussion where students can ask questions, provide feedback, and offer suggestions for improvement.

Design Challenge - Identifying a Real-World Problem
(Continued)

- Reflection and Closure (10 minutes):
  - Ask students to reflect on the process of identifying a real-world problem and the challenges they encountered.
  - Encourage them to think about how design thinking can help in finding innovative solutions to the identified problems.

Resources for Further Exploration:
- Green Education Foundation: www.greeneducationfoundation.org
- Biomimicry Institute: biomimicry.org
- Environmental Protection Agency: www.epa.gov/students

Challenge: Create an Eco-Friendly Packaging Solution

<u>Problem Statement:</u> Design and create an eco-friendly packaging solution for a common product. Your packaging should be sustainable, functional, and aesthetically appealing while minimizing environmental impact.

Design Process:

1. <u>Research:</u> Conduct research to understand the environmental impact of current packaging solutions and explore sustainable alternatives. Look for inspiration and gather ideas to inform your design.
2. <u>Brainstorming:</u> Generate ideas for your eco-friendly packaging design. Consider the product's size, shape, and protection needs. Think about how you can minimize waste, use renewable materials, or incorporate innovative features.
3. <u>Planning:</u> Sketch out your design ideas on paper. Consider different angles, features, and how the packaging will be assembled. Make sure it meets the criteria of being functional, eco-friendly, and visually appealing.
4. <u>Prototype:</u> Using the materials provided, create a prototype of your packaging design. Test different materials and construction techniques. Don't worry about it being perfect— prototypes are meant for learning and improvement.
5. <u>Evaluation:</u> Assess your prototype against the design criteria. Does it meet the requirements for sustainability, functionality, and aesthetics? Seek feedback from peers, teachers, or family members to gain different perspectives.
6. <u>Iteration:</u> Based on the feedback received, make improvements to your design. Refine your prototype, making adjustments to materials, structure, or visual elements. Don't be afraid to experiment and take risks.
7. <u>Presentation:</u> Prepare a short presentation to showcase your eco-friendly packaging solution. Explain the problem you were addressing, your design process, and the features of your final design. Highlight the sustainable aspects and why it stands out.

Tips:

- Think creatively and explore unconventional materials or design elements.
- Consider the entire lifecycle of the packaging, from production to disposal.
- Collaborate with your peers and learn from each other's ideas and perspectives.
- Emphasize the importance of sustainability and how your design contributes to a greener future.

Developing Solutions Using Design Thinking Principles

Objective: Guide students in developing innovative solutions to the real-world problems they identified in the previous lesson, using design thinking principles.

Materials:

- Whiteboard or chart paper
- Markers, chalk, colored pencils, or other art supplies
- Prototyping materials (paper, cardboard, fabric, etc.)
- Scissors, glue, tape

Procedure: (Day 2 of 2)

1. Review (10 minutes):
   - Recap the design challenge and the real-world problems identified by each team.
   - Remind students of the importance of empathy and user-centered design when developing solutions.
2. Ideation and Brainstorming (20 minutes):
   - Instruct each team to brainstorm possible solutions to the design challenge problem they were given.
   - Encourage them to think creatively, considering multiple ideas and variations.
   - Emphasize that quantity and diversity of ideas are more important than evaluating their feasibility at this stage.
3. Solution Selection (10 minutes):
   - Ask each team to choose one solution that they find most promising.
   - Instruct them to explain why they believe it will effectively address the identified problem.
4. Prototyping (25 minutes):
   - Provide the teams with prototyping materials, such as paper, cardboard, or fabric.
   - Instruct them to create a rough prototype or representation of their chosen solution.
   - Encourage iterative prototyping, allowing them to refine and modify their designs as they progress.
5. Testing and Feedback (15 minutes):
   - Instruct the teams to share their prototypes with another team or perform a simple test themselves.
   - Ask them to gather feedback on their solution's functionality, usability, and potential impact.
   - Encourage constructive criticism and suggestions for improvement.

Developing Solutions Using Design Thinking Principles
(Continued)

- Presentation and Reflection (10 minutes):
  - Give each team an opportunity to present their solution and explain thei design process.
  - Facilitate a class discussion where students can share their feedback and reflect on the challenges faced during prototyping and testing.
- Closure (10 minutes):
  - Summarize the key takeaways from the lesson, emphasizing the importance o prototyping, testing, and feedback in the design thinking process.
  - Encourage students to continue refining their solutions based on the feedbac received and prepare for the next stage of the design challenge.

Week 2

Introduction to Basic Scientific Concepts

Introduction to Basic Scientific Concepts

Objective: Introduce students to basic scientific concepts in physics, chemistry, and biology.

Materials:
- Whiteboard or chart paper
- Markers or chalk
- Handouts with scientific concepts and examples

Procedure:

1. Warm-up Activity (10 minutes):
   - Ask students to share examples of scientific concepts they have heard of or encountered in their daily lives.
   - Write their responses on the whiteboard or chart paper.
2. Introduction to Physics (15 minutes):
   - Define physics as the study of matter, energy, and their interactions.
   - Discuss examples of physics concepts, such as motion, forces, energy, and electricity.
   - Explain the importance of physics in various fields and its practical applications.
3. Introduction to Chemistry (15 minutes):
   - Define chemistry as the study of matter, its properties, composition, and transformations.
   - Discuss examples of chemistry concepts, such as elements, compounds, chemical reactions, and states of matter.
   - Highlight the relevance of chemistry in everyday life, industry, and environmental sustainability.
4. Introduction to Biology (15 minutes):
   - Define biology as the study of living organisms and their interactions with the environment.
   - Discuss examples of biology concepts, such as cells, genetics, ecosystems, and biodiversity.
   - Explain the significance of biology in understanding life processes, health, and ecological conservation.
5. Reflection and Closure (10 minutes):
   - Ask students to reflect on the scientific concepts discussed and identify which ones interest them the most.
   - Encourage students to share their reflections and reasons for their choices.
   - Summarize the key points discussed in the lesson and highlight the importance of scientific knowledge in various disciplines.

Science Concepts: Unlocking the Wonders of the Natural World!

- <u>Matter:</u> Matter is everything that has mass and occupies space. It can exist in different states: solid, liquid, and gas.
  Examples:
    - Ice melting into water when heated.
    - A balloon expanding when filled with air.
- <u>Energy:</u> Energy is the ability to do work. It comes in various forms, such as light, heat, sound, and electrical energy.
  Examples:
    - Sunlight providing energy for plants to perform photosynthesis.
    - A battery powering a flashlight.
- <u>Force:</u> Force is a push or a pull that can change an object's motion or shape.
  Examples:
    - Throwing a ball and watching it move through the air.
    - Pushing a door to open it.
- <u>Gravity:</u> Gravity is the force that pulls objects toward each other. It keeps us grounded on Earth and governs the motion of celestial bodies.
  Examples:
    - Dropping an object and observing it fall to the ground.
    - The Moon orbiting around the Earth due to gravitational attraction.
- <u>Cells:</u> Cells are the basic building blocks of living organisms. They perform specific functions and work together to sustain life.
  Examples:
    - Observing plant cells under a microscope.
    - Investigating the structure of human skin cells.
- <u>Ecosystem:</u> An ecosystem is a community of living organisms interacting with their physical environment. It includes plants, animals, and their surrounding habitats.
  Examples:
    - Studying a coral reef ecosystem and its diverse marine life.
    - Analyzing a forest ecosystem and the relationships between plants, animals, and decomposers.

- <u>Genetics:</u> Genetics is the study of genes and heredity, explaining how traits are passed down from parents to offspring.
  Examples:
  - Observing inherited traits like eye color or hair texture in a family.
  - Investigating genetic disorders and their causes.
- <u>Earth's Systems:</u> Earth's systems are interconnected processes that shape the planet, including the geosphere, hydrosphere, atmosphere, and biosphere.
  Examples:
  - Studying the water cycle and how it influences weather patterns.
  - Analyzing the impact of plate tectonics on earthquakes and volcanic activity.
- <u>Acids and Bases:</u> Acids and bases are substances with different pH levels that can react and neutralize each other.
  Examples:
  - Testing the pH of different household substances like lemon juice or baking soda.
  - Seeing a color change when adding an indicator to an acidic or basic solution.
- <u>Electric Circuits:</u> Electric circuits allow the flow of electricity and consist of components like batteries, wires, switches, and light bulbs.
  Examples:
  - Building a simple circuit to light up a bulb.
  - Investigating how adding more batteries affects the brightness of a bulb.

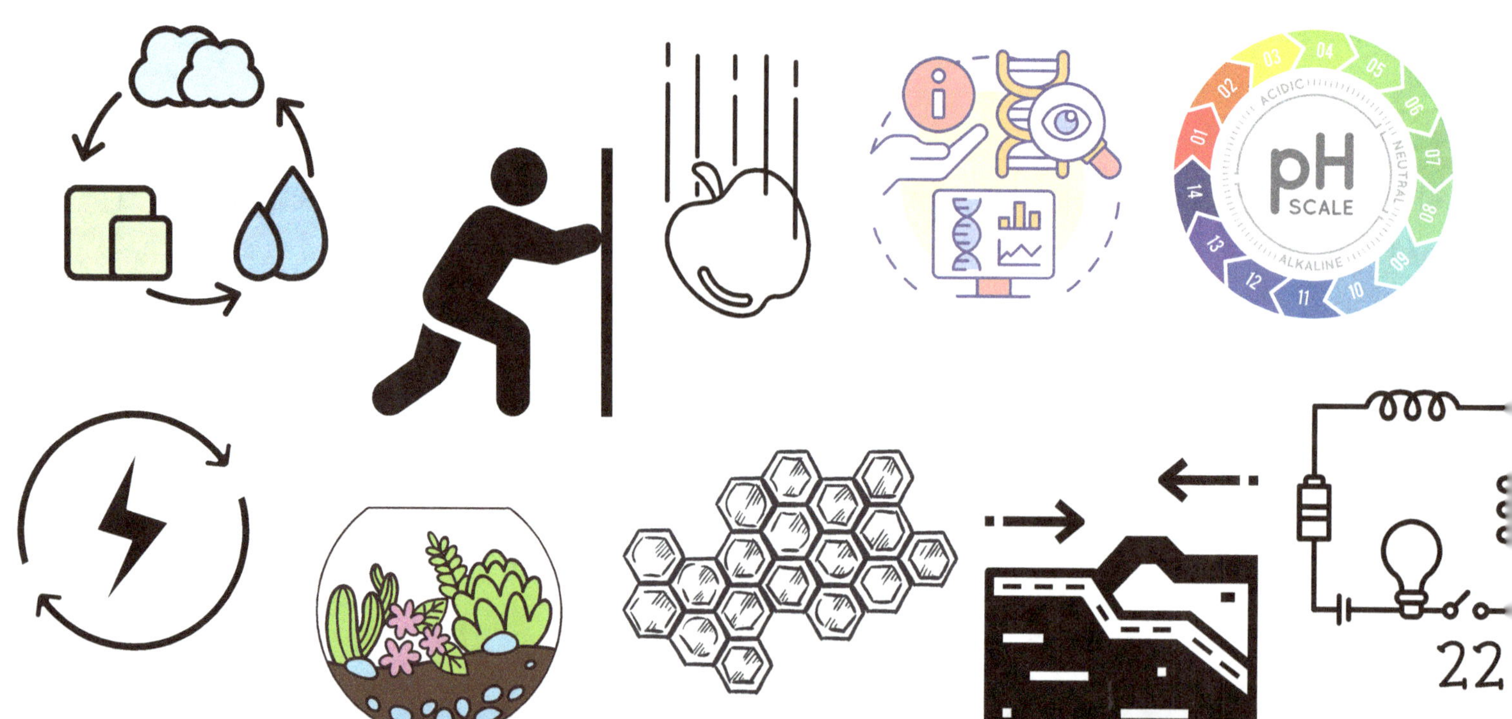

Exploration of Different Types of Technology

Objective: Introduce students to different types of technology, including coding, robotics, and electronics.

Materials:
- Whiteboard or chart paper
- Markers or chalk
- Visual aids or videos showcasing different types of technology
- Handout with different types of technology

Procedure:
1. Warm-up Activity (10 minutes):
   - Display images or videos of various technological devices and ask students to identify them.
   - Discuss their observations and experiences with different types of technology.
2. Introduction to Coding (15 minutes):
   - Explain coding as the process of creating instructions for computers and devices.
   - Discuss different programming languages and their applications.
   - Provide examples of coding in everyday life, such as mobile apps, websites, and software.
3. Introduction to Robotics (15 minutes):
   - Define robotics as the field that combines engineering and technology to create robots.
   - Discuss the various applications of robotics, such as industrial automation, healthcare, and exploration.
   - Show videos or images of different types of robots and their functionalities.
4. Introduction to Electronics (15 minutes):
   - Define electronics as the study and application of electrical circuits and devices.
   - Discuss the basics of electronic components, such as resistors, capacitors, and transistors.
   - Explain the importance of electronics in modern technology, including smartphones, computers, and renewable energy systems.

Exploration of Different Types of Technology
(Continued)

- Reflection and Closure (10 minutes):
  - Ask students to reflect on the types of technology discussed and identify which ones interest them the most.
  - Encourage students to share their reflections and reasons for their choices.
  - Summarize the key points discussed in the lesson and highlight the impact of technology on society and everyday life.

Visual Aids/Videos:
- Representing Numbers and Letters with Binary: Crash Course Computer Science #4 - https://youtu.be/1GSjbWtOc9M
- Robots: Crash Course Computer Science #37 - https://youtu.be/3XkLOqQ21Oo
- Introduction to Coding - Young Kids - https://youtu.be/y5bXW_gEJI8
- Capacitors Explained - The basics of how capacitors work working principle - https://youtu.be/X4EUwTwZ110
- Transistors Explained - How transistors work - https://youtu.be/J4oO7PT_hzQ
- DC parallel circuits explained - The basics of how parallel circuits work working principle - https://youtu.be/5uyJezQNSHw
- DC Series circuits explained - The basic working principle - https://youtu.be/VV6tZ3Aqfuc

Resources for Further Exploration:
- Code.org: www.code.org
- Robotics Education & Competition Foundation: www.roboticseducation.org
- Arduino: www.arduino.cc
- Khan Academy: www.khanacademy.org/computing/computer-science

Discover the World of Technology:
Unlocking the Power of Innovation!

- <u>Coding and Programming:</u> Coding involves writing sets of instructions (code) that computers understand. It's the backbone of software development and digital innovation.
  Examples:
    - Creating a website using HTML and CSS.
    - Developing a mobile app using languages like Python or Java.
- <u>Robotics:</u> Robotics combines engineering, electronics, and computer science to create intelligent machines that can perform tasks autonomously.
  Examples:
    - Building a robot that can navigate a maze or perform specific movements.
    - Programming a robotic arm to assemble objects.
- <u>Electronics:</u> Electronics involve designing, building, and manipulating electrical circuits to create devices that process, transmit, and store information.
  Examples:
    - Constructing a simple circuit to power an LED.
    - Designing and building a digital thermometer using sensors and microcontrollers.
- <u>Virtual Reality (VR) and Augmented Reality (AR):</u> VR creates immersive, computer-generated environments, while AR overlays digital information into the real world.
  Examples:
    - Exploring historical landmarks through a virtual reality headset.
    - Using an augmented reality app to visualize and interact with 3D models.
- <u>Internet of Things (IoT):</u> IoT refers to a network of physical objects (devices, vehicles, appliances) connected to the Internet, enabling them to collect and exchange data.
  Examples:
    - Building a smart home system that allows remote control of lights, temperature, and security.
    - Designing a wearable device that tracks health metrics and sends data to a smartphone.

- <u>3D Printing:</u> 3D printing is the process of creating three-dimensional objects by adding material layer by layer. It offers endless possibilities for rapid prototyping and manufacturing.
  Examples:
  - Designing and printing a personalized keychain or jewelry item.
  - Creating a model of a building or an anatomical structure.
- <u>Artificial Intelligence (AI):</u> AI involves creating intelligent machines that can simulate human intelligence and perform tasks that typically require human cognition.
  Examples:
  - Developing a chatbot that can answer questions and provide assistance.
  - Training a machine learning model to recognize and classify images.
- <u>Renewable Energy Technology:</u> Renewable energy technology focuses on harnessing natural resources like sunlight, wind, and water to generate clean and sustainable energy.
  Examples:
  - Designing a solar-powered car or a wind turbine.
  - Building a small-scale hydroelectric generator.
- <u>Biotechnology:</u> Biotechnology applies biological knowledge and techniques to create new products, improve agriculture, and advance medicine.
  Examples:
  - Cultivating bacteria to produce useful enzymes or antibiotics.
  - Conducting genetic engineering experiments to modify organisms.
- <u>Cybersecurity:</u> Cybersecurity involves protecting computer systems, networks, and data from unauthorized access, attacks, and breaches.
  Examples:
  - Learning about password security and encryption methods.
  - Exploring techniques to identify and prevent phishing or malware attacks.

Building and Programming Robots

Objective: Engage students in hands-on activities to build and program robots.

Materials:
- Robot kits (LEGO Mindstorms, VEX Robotics, etc.)
- Computers or laptops with programming software
- Handouts with building instructions and programming guides

Procedure:
1. Introduction to Robot Building (15 minutes):
   - Explain the objective of the lesson: to build and program robots using robot kits.
   - Provide an overview of the robot kits and their components.
   - Discuss the importance of following instructions and working collaboratively.
2. Robot Building Activity (30 minutes):
   - Divide students into small groups and distribute robot kits to each group.
   - Provide handouts with building instructions for a basic robot design.
   - Instruct the groups to follow the instructions and build their robots.
3. Introduction to Robot Programming (15 minutes):
   - Introduce the programming software used for the robot kits.
   - Explain the basics of programming, including commands, loops, and sensors.
   - Demonstrate how to program a simple task, such as making the robot move forward and backward.
4. Robot Programming Activity (30 minutes):
   - Instruct the groups to connect their robots to the computers or laptops.
   - Provide handouts with programming challenges or tasks for the robots.
   - Guide the students in programming their robots to complete the tasks using the programming software.
5. Reflection and Closure (10 minutes):
   - Ask each group to share their experiences, challenges, and successes in building and programming the robots.
   - Facilitate a class discussion on the importance of problem-solving, perseverance, and critical thinking in the robot-building process.

Robot Kits:
- LEGO Mindstorms - https://www.lego.com/en-us/product/robot-inventor-51515
- VEX Robotics - https://www.vexrobotics.com/iq-bundles.html

Conducting Science Experiments and Creating Circuits

Objective: Engage students in hands-on activities to conduct science experiments and create circuits.

Materials:

- Science experiment materials (beakers, test tubes, chemicals, etc.)
- Circuit components (Battery (1.5V AA or AAA), Light bulb (preferably an LED bulb), Electrical wires with alligator clips, Cardboard or foam board, and Safety goggles)

Procedure:

1. Introduction to Science Experiments (15 minutes):
   - Explain the objective of the lesson: to conduct science experiments and explore scientific principles.
   - Provide an overview of the science experiment materials and safety precautions.
   - Discuss the scientific method and the importance of accurate measurements and observations.
2. Science Experiment Activity (30 minutes):
   - Divide students into small groups and provide them with science experiment materials.
   - Instruct the groups to follow the experiment procedures and record their observations and results.
3. Introduction to Circuit Creation (15 minutes):
   - Introduce the basics of circuits, including components and their functions.
   - Demonstrate how to create a simple circuit using foam board, wires, and an LED.
   - Discuss safety precautions when working with circuits and electricity.
4. Circuit Creation Activity (30 minutes):
   - Instruct the groups to gather circuit components and set up their workstations.
   - Provide handouts or circuit diagrams for different projects (e.g., light-up cards, burglar alarms).
   - Guide the students in creating and testing their circuits, ensuring proper connections and functionality.
5. Reflection and Closure (10 minutes):
   - Ask each group to share their experiences, challenges, and discoveries during the science experiments and circuit creation.
   - Facilitate a class discussion on the importance of observation, precision, and troubleshooting in science and electronics.

Safety Rules
(Given before experiment begins)

1. <u>Adult Supervision:</u> Always have an adult present when conducting the experiment. They can guide you, provide assistance, and ensure safety precautions are followed.
2. <u>Safety Goggles:</u> Wear safety goggles to protect your eyes from potential hazards, such as sparks or loose wires.
3. <u>Low Voltage Power Source:</u> Use batteries with low voltage, such as 1.5V AA or AAA batteries, for simple circuits. Avoid using high-voltage power sources to minimize the risk of electrical shock.
4. <u>Check for Damage:</u> Inspect all equipment, wires, batteries, and components before use. Do not use damaged or frayed wires, and replace any faulty components.
5. <u>Disconnect Power:</u> Make sure the circuit is disconnected from the power source (batteries) before making any adjustments or modifications. This helps prevent accidental electrical shocks or short circuits.
6. <u>Dry Working Area:</u> Keep your work area dry and avoid conducting experiments near water sources to minimize the risk of electrical shock.
7. <u>Secure Connections:</u> Follow the circuit diagram carefully and ensure all wire connections are secure. Avoid loose or exposed wires that could cause short circuits or sparks.
8. <u>Turn Off When Not in Use:</u> Turn off the circuit or disconnect the power source when you are not actively working with it. This helps prevent accidental contact and reduces the risk of electrical hazards.
9. <u>No Touching:</u> Do not touch any part of the circuit while it is connected to a power source. Even low-voltage circuits can cause tingling or mild shocks.
10. <u>Organized Workspace:</u> Keep your work area clean and organized. Avoid clutter and tangled wires, which can lead to accidents or confusion.
11. <u>Fire Safety:</u> Keep flammable materials away from the circuit. Do not place the circuit near flammable liquids, gases, or materials that could ignite easily.
12. <u>Follow Instructions:</u> Read and follow the experiment instructions carefully. Do not deviate from the procedure unless instructed by an adult or teacher.
13. <u>Report Accidents:</u> In case of accidents, such as electrical shocks or injuries, immediately inform an adult or teacher.

(Experiment) Let There Be Light: Creating a Simple Circuit

Procedure:

1. <u>Safety First:</u> Put on your safety goggles to protect your eyes during the experiment.
2. <u>Gather Your Materials:</u> Collect all the necessary materials and arrange them on a clean and flat surface.
3. <u>Understand the Components:</u> Familiarize yourself with the battery, light bulb, and electrical wires. Observe the positive (+) and negative (-) terminals on the battery and the corresponding terminals on the light bulb.
4. <u>Create the Circuit:</u> a) Take the cardboard or foam board and arrange the battery and light bulb on it. Ensure they are stable and won't move during the experiment. b) Connect one end of an electrical wire to the positive (+) terminal of the battery. Use an alligator clip to secure the connection. c) Attach the other end of the same wire to the longer leg of the light bulb. Secure the connection with an alligator clip. d) Connect a second wire to the negative (-) terminal of the battery using an alligator clip. e) Attach the other end of the second wire to the shorter leg of the light bulb. Secure the connection with an alligator clip.
5. <u>Observe and Predict:</u> a) Take a moment to carefully observe the circuit you've created. Examine the connections and note the position of the bulb. b) Predict what will happen when you complete the circuit by connecting the wires to the battery.
6. <u>Complete the Circuit:</u> a) Connect the alligator clip on the wire attached to the battery's negative (-) terminal to the shorter leg of the light bulb. b) Ensure the connections are secure and no loose wires are touching each other.
7. <u>Observe and Record:</u> a) As you complete the circuit, observe the light bulb. Does it light up? b) Record your observations, noting any changes in brightness or color.
8. <u>Experiment with Different Setups:</u> a) Experiment by changing the position of the wires or swapping the connections. b) Observe the effects of these changes on the light bulb's illumination.
9. <u>Reflect and Discuss:</u> a) What do you think happens in the circuit that allows the light bulb to light up? b) How does the flow of electricity occur in a closed circuit?

<u>Safety Note:</u> Remember to disconnect the wires from the battery once you have completed your observations to avoid accidental short circuits.

Will the Bulb Light Up or Not?

Circle a ✓ if the bulb lights up and circle an ✗ if the bulb does not light up.

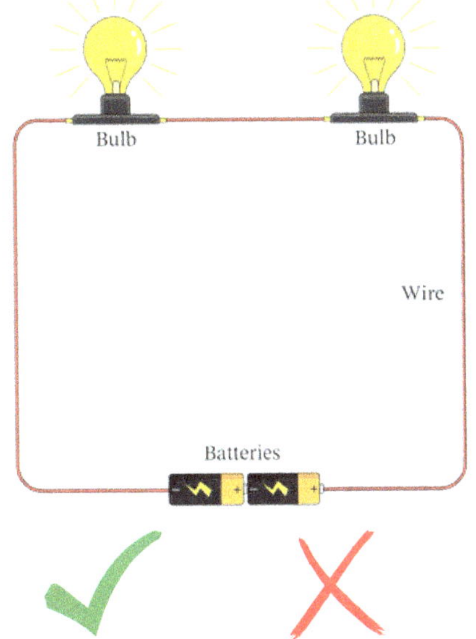

✓ ✗

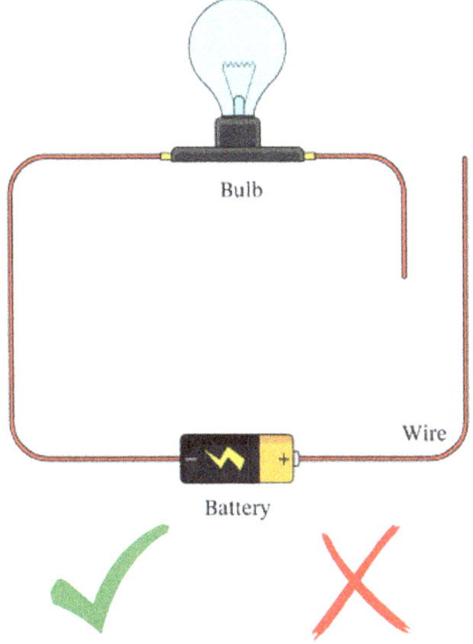

✓ ✗

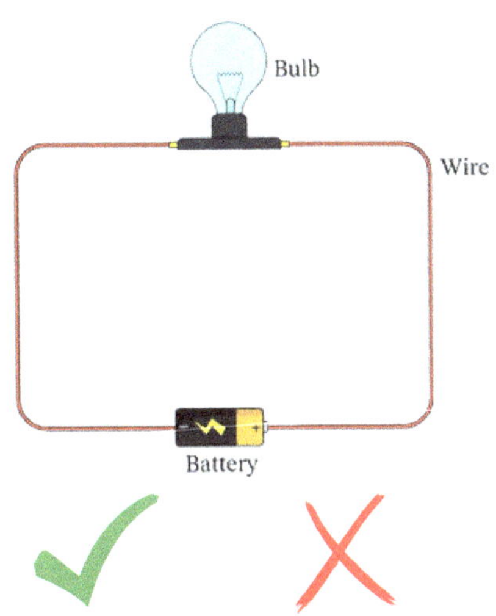

✓ ✗

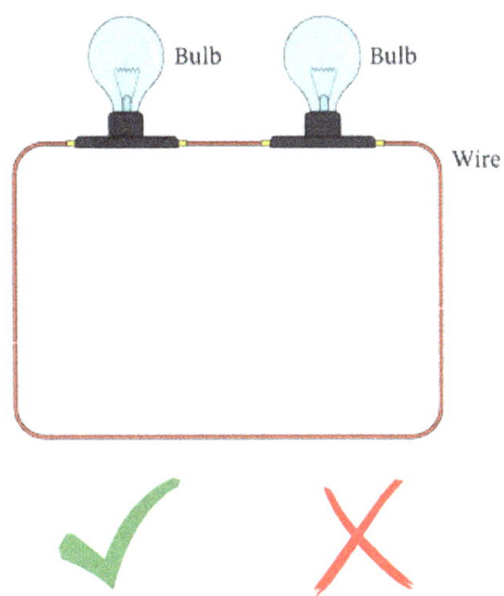

✓ ✗

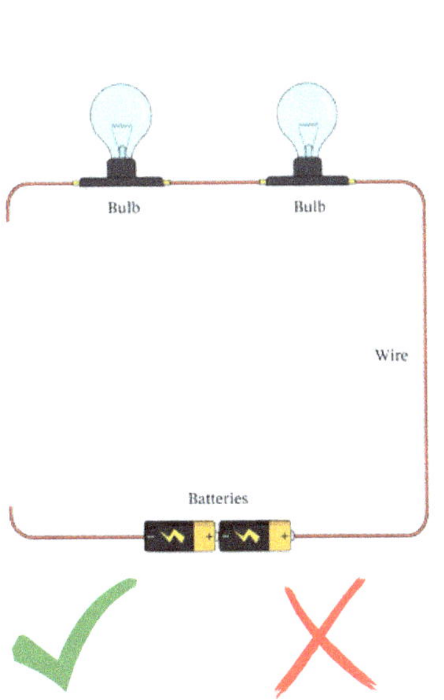

✓ ✗

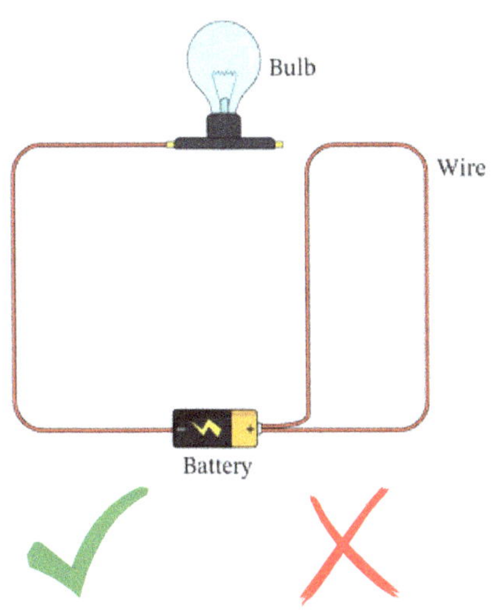

✓ ✗

Week 3

Engineering and Math

Introduction to Different Engineering Fields

Objective: Introduce students to various engineering fields, including civil, mechanical, and aerospace engineering.

Materials:

- Whiteboard or chart paper
- Markers or chalk
- Handouts with information on different engineering fields

Procedure:

1. Warm-up Activity (10 minutes):
   - Display images or videos of different engineering projects (bridges, cars, airplanes, etc.).
   - Ask students to identify the engineering fields associated with each project.
   - Discuss their responses as a class.
2. Introduction to Engineering Fields (15 minutes):
   - Explain the concept of engineering and its importance in solving real-world problems.
   - Introduce civil engineering, mechanical engineering, and aerospace engineering as examples of different engineering fields.
   - Discuss the applications and typical projects associated with each field.
3. Civil Engineering (15 minutes):
   - Explain civil engineering as the branch that focuses on the design and construction of infrastructure and buildings.
   - Discuss examples of civil engineering projects, such as bridges, dams, and skyscrapers.
   - Highlight the role of civil engineers in ensuring the safety and sustainability of structures.
4. Mechanical Engineering (15 minutes):
   - Explain mechanical engineering as the branch that deals with the design and development of mechanical systems and machines.
   - Discuss examples of mechanical engineering projects, such as cars, robots, and engines.
   - Emphasize the importance of mechanical engineers in improving efficiency and solving mechanical problems.

Introduction to Different Engineering Fields
(Continued)

- Aerospace Engineering (15 minutes):
  - Explain aerospace engineering as the branch that focuses on the design and development of aircraft and spacecraft.
  - Discuss examples of aerospace engineering projects, such as airplanes, satellites, and rockets.
  - Highlight the role of aerospace engineers in advancing space exploration and aviation technology.
- Reflection and Closure (10 minutes):
  - Ask students to reflect on the engineering fields discussed and identify which ones interest them the most.
  - Encourage students to share their reflections and reasons for their choices.
  - Summarize the key points discussed in the lesson and highlight the diverse opportunities available in engineering.

Resources for Further Exploration:
- What is Engineering?: Crash Course Engineering #1 - https://youtu.be/btGYcizV0iI
- Civil Engineering: Crash Course Engineering #2 - https://youtu.be/-xbtnz4wdaA
- Mechanical Engineering: Crash Course Engineering #3 - https://youtu.be/A1V-QQ5wFU4
- Biomedical & Industrial Engineering: Crash Course Engineering #6 - https://youtu.be/O6lENrRANxY

Engineering Fields: Exploring the World of Innovation

- Mechanical Engineering:
  - Mechanical engineers design and create machines and mechanical systems.
  - Examples: Engines, vehicles, robots, manufacturing equipment.
- Civil Engineering:
  - Civil engineers plan, design, and construct infrastructure projects that benefit society.
  - Examples: Bridges, buildings, roads, dams, and water supply systems.
- Electrical Engineering:
  - Electrical engineers work with electrical systems and develop technologies that harness and control electricity.
  - Examples: Power grids, circuits, electrical devices, telecommunications systems.
- Aerospace Engineering:
  - Aerospace engineers design, develop, and test aircraft and spacecraft.
  - Examples: Airplanes, satellites, rockets, drones.
- Chemical Engineering:
  - Chemical engineers apply principles of chemistry and engineering to create and optimize chemical processes.
  - Examples: Chemical plants, pharmaceuticals, food processing.
- Environmental Engineering:
  - Environmental engineers focus on developing sustainable solutions to protect and improve the environment.
  - Examples: Waste management systems, water treatment plants, and renewable energy systems.
- Biomedical Engineering:
  - Biomedical engineers combine engineering principles with medical knowledge to design and develop healthcare technologies.
  - Examples: Prosthetics, medical devices, imaging systems.
- Computer Engineering:
  - Computer engineers design and develop computer hardware and software systems.
  - Examples: Computer processors, computer networks, and software applications.

- <u>Materials Engineering:</u>
  - Materials engineers study and develop new materials with improved properties for various applications.
  - Examples: Metals, ceramics, polymers, composites.
- <u>Industrial Engineering:</u>
  - Industrial engineers optimize complex systems to increase efficiency and productivity.
  - Examples: Supply chains, manufacturing processes, logistics.

Math Activities and Games to Reinforce Concepts
(Day 1)

Objective: Engage students in math activities and games to reinforce concepts such as geometry, and algebra.

Materials:

- Whiteboard, chart paper, construction paper, different colored strips of paper
- Markers or chalk
- Math activity handouts
- Math-related games or manipulatives
- Math concept-related visual aids or videos
- Scissors and glue
- Laptops (either enough for students to work in pairs or individually)

Procedure:

1. Warm-up Activity (10 minutes):
   - Write the math riddle on the board (labeled Lesson Riddle)
   - Ask students to spend some time trying to solve the riddle given. They can work individually or in pairs.
   - Discuss the solution as a class.

2. Geometry Activity (20 minutes):
   - Introduce the geometry concept; angles.
   - Provide handouts or worksheets with geometry problems or exercises.
   - Instruct students to work individually or in pairs to solve the problems.

3. Algebra Activity (20 minutes):
   - Introduce the website IXL and show students where they will be exploring.
   - Provide students with a laptop to work individually or in pairs.
   - Ask students to explore different grade-level appropriate math topics.

4. Math Games or Manipulatives (20 minutes): Optional
   - Engage students in math-related games or manipulative activities.
   - Provide math puzzles, board games, or manipulatives like pattern blocks or tangrams.
   - Allow students to work individually or in small groups to reinforce math concepts in a fun and interactive way.

Math Activities and Games to Reinforce Concepts
(Day 1 - Continued)

- Reflection and Closure (10 minutes):
  - Ask students to reflect on the math activities and games they participated in.
  - Discuss the challenges they encountered and the strategies they used to solve problems.
  - Summarize the key math concepts covered and highlight the importance of math in engineering and problem-solving.

Lesson Video(s) and website(s):
- Types of Angles | Acute, Right, Obtuse, Straight, Reflex, & Complete - https://youtu.be/IxkqJc3P40E
- https://www.ixl.com/math

How do you go from 98 to 720 using just one letter?

A: Add an "x" between "ninety" and "eight". Ninety x Eight = 720

If you have extra time, here are some extra riddles for more math fun!

A merchant can place 8 large boxes or 10 small boxes into a carton for shipping. In one shipment, he sent a total of 96 boxes. If there are more large boxes than small boxes, how many cartons did he ship?

A: 11 cartons total
7 large boxes (7 * 8 = 56 boxes)
4 small boxes (4 10 = 40 boxes
11 total cartons and 96 boxes

A duck was given $9, a spider was given $36, and a bee was given $27. Based on this information, how much money would be given to a cat?

A: $18 ($4.50 per leg)

Abstract Angles

Directions:

1. Have students <u>cut out the label cards and</u> set them aside.
2. <u>Glue the name card in a corner</u> of the background sheet.
3. <u>Lay out colored strips to form angles.</u>
4. <u>Glue on labels.</u> Again, this was new for my students when we made these, so I checked their work before allowing them to glue.

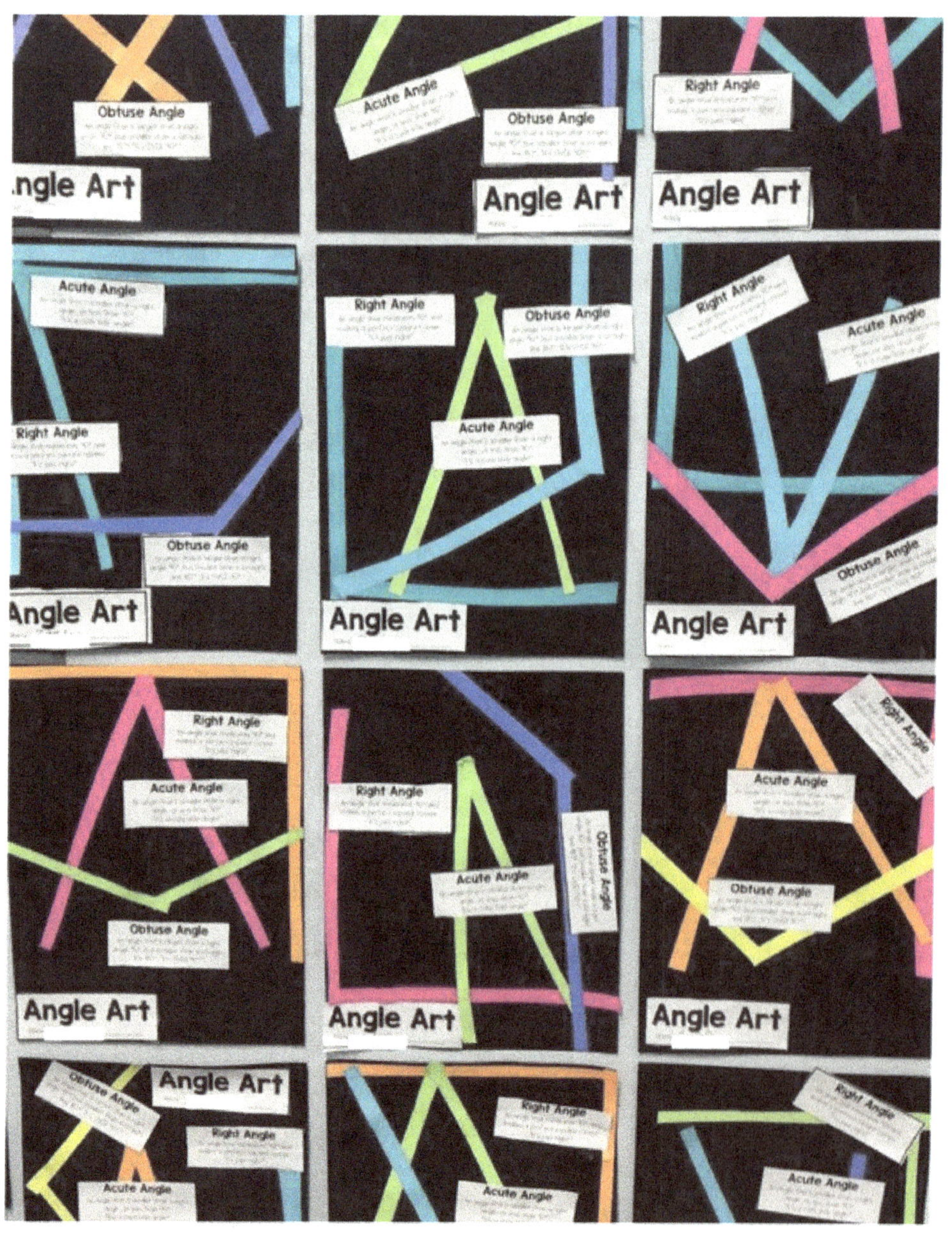

Can be completed in a whole group, small groups, or independently

Angle Art

Name: ___________________________

Angle Art

Name: ___________________________

Right Angle

An angle that measures 90° and makes a perfect square corner. "It's just right!"

Right Angle

An angle that measures 90° and makes a perfect square corner. "It's just right!"

Acute Angle

An angle that's smaller than a right angle or less than 90°. "It's a cute little angle!"

Acute Angle

An angle that's smaller than a right angle or less than 90°. "It's a cute little angle!"

Obtuse Angle

An angle that is larger than a right angle (90°), but smaller than a straight line (180°). "It's OVER 90°."

Obtuse Angle

An angle that is larger than a right angle (90°), but smaller than a straight line (180°). "It's OVER 90°."

Types of Angles: Exploring the World of Geometry

1. Acute Angle:
   - An acute angle is less than 90 degrees.
   - It is like a "small" angle that appears sharp.
   - Examples: The angle formed when you fold a piece of paper or the angle at the tip of a pencil.
2. Right Angle:
   - A right angle measures exactly 90 degrees.
   - It forms a square corner and is often represented by a small square symbol (L).
   - Examples: The corners of most books, the corners of a table or a classroom whiteboard.
3. Obtuse Angle:
   - An obtuse angle is greater than 90 degrees but less than 180 degrees.
   - It is like a "wide" angle that appears open.
   - Examples: The angle formed by a partially opened door or the angle between two walls in a room.
4. Straight Angle:
   - A straight angle measures exactly 180 degrees.
   - It forms a straight line and is often represented by a straight line symbol (—).
   - Examples: The angle formed by a folded ruler or the angle along a line segment.
5. Reflex Angle:
   - A reflex angle is greater than 180 degrees but less than 360 degrees.
   - It is like an "extended" angle that goes beyond a straight line.
   - Examples: The angle formed by the minute hand and the hour hand of a clock when it is between two hours.
6. Complementary Angles:
   - Complementary angles are two angles that add up to 90 degrees.
   - They "complete" each other to form a right angle.
   - Example: If one angle measures 30 degrees, the complementary angle will measure 60 degrees.
7. Supplementary Angles:
   - Supplementary angles are two angles that add up to 180 degrees.
   - They "supplement" each other to form a straight line.
   - Example: If one angle measures 120 degrees, the supplementary angle will measure 60 degrees.

Math Activities and Games to Reinforce Concepts
(Day 2)

Objective: Continue engaging students in math activities and games to reinforce concepts such as geometry, and algebra.

Materials:
- Whiteboard or chart paper
- Markers or chalk
- Math activity handouts
- Math-related games or manipulatives
- Laptops (either enough for students to work in pairs or individually)

Procedure:
1. Warm-up Activity (10 minutes):
    - Write the math riddle on the board (labeled Lesson Riddle)
    - Ask students to solve the riddle individually or in pairs.
    - Discuss the solution as a class.
2. Geometry Activity (20 minutes):
    - Review the geometry concept from the previous day.
    - Provide additional handouts or worksheets with geometry problems or exercises.
    - Instruct students to work individually or in pairs to solve the problems.
3. Algebra Activity (20 minutes):
    - Review how to access the IXL website and where students explored the previous day.
    - Provide students with a laptop to work individually or in pairs.
    - Ask students to explore different grade-level appropriate math topics.
4. Math Games or Manipulatives (20 minutes): Optional
    - Continue engaging students in math-related games or manipulative activities.
    - Provide different math puzzles, board games, or manipulatives like pattern blocks or tangrams.
    - Allow students to work individually or in small groups to reinforce math concepts in a fun and interactive way.

Math Activities and Games to Reinforce Concepts
(Day 2 - Continued)

- Reflection and Closure (10 minutes):
    - Ask students to reflect on the math activities and games from both days.
    - Discuss the overall challenges they encountered and the strategies they used to solve problems.
    - Summarize the key math concepts covered throughout the two days and emphasize their relevance in various fields, such as engineering and problem-solving.

Note: The specific concepts, problems, and games can be adjusted based on the grade level and prior knowledge of the students.

How do you make the number 7 even without addition, subtraction, multiplication, or division?

A: Drop the "S"

f you have extra time, here are some extra riddles for more math fun!

Write down the next number in the pattern: 2, 3, 5, 8, 13...

A: 21

When my dad was 31, I was just 8 years old. Now his age is twice as old as my age. What is my present age?

A: When you calculate the difference between the ages, you can see that it is 23 years. So you must be 23 years old now.

What number do you get when you multiply all of the numbers on a telephone's number pad?

A: Zero, because any number multiplied by 0 will always equal 0.

Design Challenge - Structure Design

Objective: Engage students in a design challenge where they work in teams to design and build a structure using engineering principles.

Materials:

- Building materials (e.g., popsicle sticks, straws, cardboard, tape, glue, pennies, aluminum foil, etc.)
- Rulers or measuring tools
- Design challenge handouts or cards
- Safety guidelines for construction

Procedure:

1. Introduction to the Design Challenge (10 minutes):
   - Explain the design challenge objective: to design and build a structure using engineering principles.
   - Provide the design challenge handouts or cards to each team.
   - Discuss the requirements and constraints of the challenge.
2. Brainstorming and Planning (15 minutes):
   - Instruct the teams to brainstorm and discuss possible design ideas for their structure.
   - Encourage them to consider factors such as stability, strength, and aesthetics.
   - Guide the teams in creating a rough sketch or plan for their structure.
3. Structure Design and Construction (40 minutes):
   - Distribute the building materials to each team.
   - Instruct them to start designing and constructing their structure based on their plan.
   - Encourage teams to work collaboratively, assigning roles and responsibilities.
4. Testing and Evaluation (15 minutes):
   - Instruct each team to test their structure for stability and strength.
   - Guide them in evaluating their design based on the design challenge requirements.
   - Encourage teams to make modifications or improvements to their structure if necessary.
5. Presentations and Reflection (20 minutes):
   - Give each team an opportunity to present their structure to the class.
   - Instruct them to explain their design process, challenges faced, and lessons learned.
   - Facilitate a class discussion where students can provide feedback and ask questions about the different structures.

Design Challenge - Structure Design
(Continued)

- Reflection and Closure (10 minutes):
  - Ask students to reflect on the design challenge experience and the engineering principles they applied.
  - Discuss the importance of collaboration, problem-solving, and creativity in engineering design.
  - Summarize the key takeaways from the lesson and highlight the connection between engineering, math, and problem-solving skills.

Safety Guidelines
(Given before experiment begins)

1. Adult Supervision: Always have adult supervision when engaging in construction activities. An experienced adult can provide guidance and ensure safety precautions are followed.
2. Safety Gear: Wear appropriate safety gear, including goggles, gloves, and closed-toe shoes, to protect your eyes, hands, and feet from potential hazards.
3. Tool Use:
   - Use tools only under adult supervision and after receiving proper instructions on how to handle them safely.
   - Handle tools with care, avoiding swinging or throwing them.
   - Return tools to their designated places after use to prevent accidents.
4. Workspace Organization:
   - Keep your work area clean and organized.
   - Remove any obstacles or clutter that may pose a tripping hazard.
   - Securely store construction materials to prevent them from falling or causing injuries.
5. Communication:
   - Clear communication is essential during construction projects.
   - Use hand signals or agreed-upon verbal cues to coordinate tasks with other team members.
6. Report Hazards:
   - Inform an adult immediately if you notice any unsafe conditions or hazards.
   - Speak up if you see someone engaging in unsafe practices.

Engineering Principles

Identify the Problem

What is the challenge?
What are the limits?
How can you solve it?

Explore

Find out what others have done. Gather materials and play with them.

Design

Think up lots of ideas. Pick one and make a plan. Make a drawing or a model.

Create

Use your plan to build your idea.

Try it out

Test your idea.

Make it Better

Think about how your design can be improved. Modify your design and try again.

Design Challenge Task Cards

Copy and cut out before distributing to students

Build a Straw Bridge

Using tape and no more than 20 straws, design a bridge that can span a gap of about 1 foot (at least 25 cm) and support as many pennies as possible.

Strong Paper Structure

Build a newspaper structure that is strong enough to hold heavy books.

Build the tallest tower possible using two different materials.

Construct a boat that floats.

Can your boat support 5 pennies without sinking?

Create a pair of glasses that will protect your eyes from the sun.

Build a device or structure that will protect a book from the rain.

Build something that flies using at least 3 different materials.

Construct a musical instrument.

Construct a free-standing 3D model of your name.

Create a bouquet of flowers using any materials.

Week 4

Arts and Creativity

Introduction to Different Forms of Art

Objective: Introduce students to different forms of art, including drawing, painting, sculpture, and music.

Materials:
- Examples of artwork (images, sculptures, musical instruments, etc.)
- Whiteboard or chart paper
- Markers or chalk

Procedure:
1. Warm-up Activity (10 minutes):
   - Display images or examples of different forms of art.
   - Ask students to identify and describe the art forms they see.
   - Discuss their responses as a class.
2. Introduction to Drawing (15 minutes):
   - Explain drawing as the art of creating images or designs using lines and shapes.
   - Discuss different drawing techniques, such as sketching, shading, and perspective.
   - Show examples of drawings by different artists and discuss their styles.
3. Introduction to Painting (15 minutes):
   - Explain painting as the art of applying pigments to a surface to create images or designs.
   - Discuss different painting techniques, such as watercolors, acrylics, and oils.
   - Show examples of paintings by different artists and discuss their styles.
4. Introduction to Sculpture (15 minutes):
   - Explain sculpture as the art of creating three-dimensional forms using materials such as clay, wood, or metal.
   - Discuss different sculpture techniques, such as carving, modeling, and assemblage.
   - Show examples of sculptures by different artists and discuss their styles.
5. Introduction to Music (15 minutes):
   - Explain music as the art of creating and expressing sounds and rhythms.
   - Discuss different musical instruments and genres.
   - Play examples of music from different styles or cultures and discuss their characteristics.

- Reflection and Closure (10 minutes):
  - Ask students to reflect on the different forms of art discussed and identify which ones interest them the most.
  - Encourage students to share their reflections and reasons for their choices.
  - Summarize the key points discussed in the lesson and highlight the importance of art in self-expression and cultural appreciation.

Exploration of How STEAM and Creativity Intersect

Objective: Explore the intersection of STEAM (Science, Technology, Engineering, Arts, and Mathematics) and creativity.

Materials:

- Whiteboard or chart paper
- Markers or chalk
- Handouts with information on STEAM and creativity

Procedure:

1. Warm-up Activity (10 minutes):
   - Ask students to brainstorm and share examples of how creativity is used in different STEAM disciplines (science, technology, engineering, arts, mathematics).
   - Write their responses on the whiteboard or chart paper.
2. Introduction to STEAM and Creativity (15 minutes):
   - Define STEAM as the integration of science, technology, engineering, arts, and mathematics.
   - Discuss the importance of creativity in STEAM disciplines and problem-solving.
   - Provide examples of how creativity is applied in various STEAM fields.
3. Creative Applications in Science and Technology (15 minutes):
   - Discuss examples of how creativity is used in scientific research, inventions, and technological innovations.
   - Highlight the role of creative thinking in problem-solving, experimental design, and hypothesis formulation.
4. Creative Applications in Engineering and Mathematics (15 minutes):
   - Discuss examples of how creativity is used in engineering design, architectural structures, and mathematical problem-solving.
   - Highlight the role of creative problem-solving, visualization, and critical thinking in engineering and mathematics.
5. Creative Applications in the Arts (15 minutes):
   - Discuss examples of how creativity is expressed through visual arts, music, dance, and theater.
   - Highlight the role of artistic creativity in self-expression, storytelling, and cultural exploration.

- Reflection and Closure (10 minutes):
  - Ask students to reflect on the intersection of STEAM and creativity.
  - Discuss how creativity enhances innovation, critical thinking, and interdisciplinary collaboration.
  - Summarize the key points discussed in the lesson and emphasize the importance of nurturing creativity in STEAM education

Resources:
- National Science Foundation: www.nsf.gov
- Edutopia: www.edutopia.org
- STEAM-Powered Classroom: www.steampoweredclassroom.com
- National Science Teaching Association: www.nsta.org

Unleashing Creativity in STEAM: Explore the Power of Innovation!

STEAM is an exciting approach that integrates Science, Technology, Engineering, Arts, and Mathematics. It's a world of endless possibilities that combines creativity with critical thinking. Let's dive into the fascinating realm of STEAM and discover how creativity plays a vital role!

What is STEAM? STEAM is a way of learning and problem-solving that brings together multiple disciplines. It encourages students to think creatively, collaborate, and explore innovative solutions to real-world challenges.
Why is Creativity Important in STEAM? Creativity is the fuel that ignites the STEAM engine. It allows you to:

1. Innovate: Think beyond boundaries and come up with new ideas and concepts.
2. Solve Problems: Tackle challenges using unique approaches and inventive thinking.
3. Express Yourself: Use art, design, and storytelling to convey your ideas and findings.
4. Design Solutions: Develop innovative solutions that improve our lives and make a positive impact.
5. Think Critically: Analyze problems from different angles and discover imaginative solutions.
6. Collaborate: Work with others, combining diverse perspectives to create something extraordinary.

STEAM and Creativity:

1. Science:
   - Scientific exploration encourages curiosity and creativity.
   - Scientists think creatively to design experiments and make new discoveries.
2. Technology:
   - Technology provides tools for creative expression and problem-solving.
   - Creative coding, designing apps, and developing digital art are examples of blending technology and creativity.
3. Engineering:
   - Engineering involves designing, building, and creating innovative solutions.
   - Engineers think creatively to develop new technologies, design sustainable structures, and solve practical problems.
4. Arts:
   - Arts inspire creativity and encourage self-expression.
   - Artists use their imagination to create visual arts, music, dance, theater, and more.
5. Mathematics:
   - Mathematics requires creative thinking to solve complex problems.
   - Math is the language of patterns and shapes, fostering creativity in problem-solving and logical reasoning.

How to Foster Creativity in STEAM:

1. Embrace Curiosity: Ask questions, explore, and be curious about the world around you.
2. Be Open-Minded: Welcome different ideas, perspectives, and possibilities.
3. Take Risks: Don't be afraid to try new things and experiment with innovative approaches.
4. Think Outside the Box: Challenge traditional thinking and explore unconventional solutions.
5. Engage in Arts and Design: Integrate arts and design elements into your STEAM projects.
6. Collaborate and Communicate: Share ideas, work in teams, and learn from others.
7. Persist and Iterate: Embrace setbacks as learning opportunities and keep refining your ideas.
8. Emphasize Playfulness: Have fun while exploring and experimenting with STEAM concepts.
9. Seek Inspiration: Explore STEAM-related books, websites, museums, and real-world applications.
10. Embrace Failure as Learning: View mistakes as stepping stones to success and keep trying.

Remember, creativity is a superpower that every STEAM explorer possesses. It allows you to push boundaries, imagine new possibilities, and shape the world around you. So, let your creativity soar as you embark on your STEAM journey!

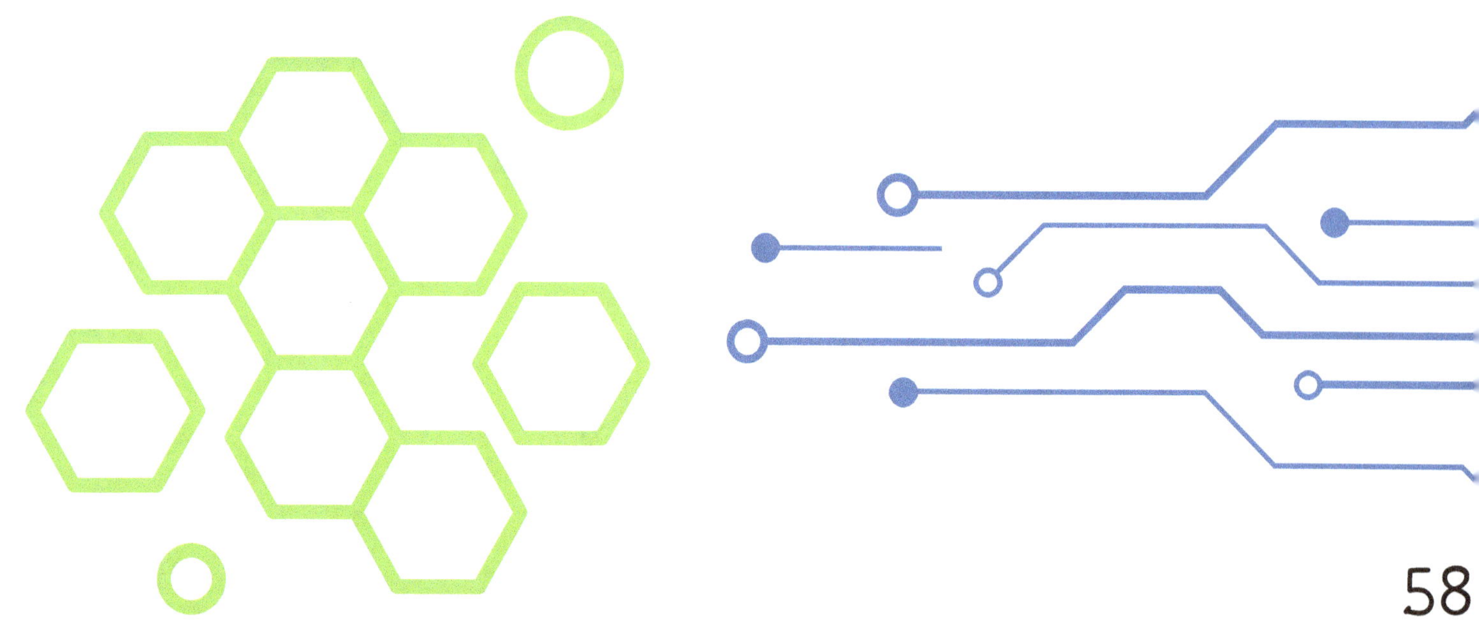

STEAM Collage

Objective: Explore the intersection of STEAM and creativity by creating a collage that represents the integration of science, technology, engineering, arts, and mathematics.

Materials:
- Magazines or printed images
- Scissors
- Glue sticks
- Construction paper or poster board
- Markers or colored pencils

Procedure:

1. Introduction (10 minutes):
   - Begin the lesson by discussing the concept of STEAM (Science, Technology, Engineering, Arts, and Mathematics) and the importance of creativity in each discipline.
   - Explain that students will create a collage that represents the integration of these subjects.
2. Brainstorming and Theme Selection (15 minutes):
   - Facilitate a brainstorming session where students generate ideas for the theme of their collages.
   - Encourage them to think about how different STEAM disciplines can be connected and integrated.
   - Provide prompts and examples if needed.
3. Gathering Materials (15 minutes):
   - Distribute magazines or printed images to students.
   - Instruct them to search for images and text that relate to their chosen theme.
   - Remind students to select a variety of images that represent different aspects of STEAM.
4. Collage Creation (30 minutes):
   - Provide construction paper or poster board for the base of the collages.
   - Instruct students to cut out the images and text that they collected and arrange them on the base.
   - Encourage them to use color, shape, and placement to create an aesthetically pleasing composition.

- Reflection and Discussion (15 minutes):
    - Ask students to reflect on their collages and how they represent the intersection of STEAM and creativity.
    - Have students share their collages with the class, explaining the connections they made between the different disciplines.
    - Facilitate a class discussion about the various ways in which STEAM and creativity intersect.
- Extension Activity (optional):
    - If time allows, have students write a brief reflection or artist statement to accompany their collages, explaining the thought process and symbolism behind their choices.
- Reflection and Closure (10 minutes):
    - Conclude the lesson by asking students to reflect on what they learned about the intersection of STEAM and creativity through the collage activity.
    - Discuss how creativity enhances problem-solving, innovation, and interdisciplinary thinking in STEAM fields.

STEAM-Inspired Invention (OPTIONAL)

Objective: Explore the intersection of STEAM and creativity by designing and prototyping a STEAM-inspired invention.

Materials:
- Design materials (paper, pencils, markers, etc.)
- Prototyping materials (cardboard, craft supplies, tape, etc.)
- Optional: Computers or tablets for research

Procedure:

1. Introduction (10 minutes):
   - Begin the lesson by discussing the relationship between STEAM and creativity, emphasizing how creativity plays a vital role in the innovation and design process.
   - Explain that students will have the opportunity to design and prototype their own STEAM-inspired inventions.
2. Brainstorming and Research (20 minutes):
   - Facilitate a brainstorming session where students generate ideas for their inventions.
   - Encourage them to consider how different STEAM disciplines can be integrated into their designs.
   - If available, provide access to computers or tablets for students to conduct research on existing inventions and STEAM-related concepts.
3. Design and Planning (20 minutes):
   - Provide students with design materials, such as paper, pencils, and markers.
   - Instruct them to sketch and label their inventions, including the various STEAM elements incorporated.
   - Encourage students to think about the functionality, features, and potential impact of their inventions.
4. Prototyping (40 minutes):
   - Provide prototyping materials, such as cardboard, craft supplies, and tape.
   - Instruct students to create a physical prototype of their invention based on their design sketches.
   - Encourage them to be resourceful and innovative in utilizing the available materials.

- Presentation and Feedback (15 minutes):
  - Allow students to present their inventions to the class.
  - Instruct them to explain the STEAM elements incorporated and the purpose of their invention.
  - Encourage classmates to provide constructive feedback and suggestions, and ask questions about the designs.
- Reflection and Discussion (15 minutes):
  - Lead a reflection session where students discuss the process of designing and prototyping their STEAM-inspired inventions.
  - Prompt them to reflect on how creativity influenced their problem-solving, critical thinking, and interdisciplinary approach.
  - Facilitate a class discussion about the various ways in which STEAM and creativity intersect in the invention process.
- Reflection and Closure (10 minutes):
  - Conclude the lesson by asking students to reflect on what they learned about the intersection of STEAM and creativity through the invention activity.
  - Discuss how creativity fosters innovation, collaboration, and real-world application of STEAM concepts.

Creative Project - Multimedia Presentation

Objective: Engage students in a creative project where they work in teams to create a multimedia presentation based on a STEAM-related theme.

Materials:
- Computers or laptops with presentation software
- Multimedia resources (images, videos, audio clips, etc.)
- Design challenge handouts or cards

Procedure:

1. Introduction to the Creative Project (10 minutes):
   - Explain the objective of the creative project: to create a multimedia presentation based on a STEAM-related theme.
   - Provide the design challenge handouts or cards to each team.
   - Discuss the requirements and expectations of the project.
2. Brainstorming and Planning (15 minutes):
   - Instruct the teams to brainstorm and discuss possible STEAM-related themes for their presentation.
   - Encourage them to consider the integration of science, technology, engineering, arts, and mathematics.
   - Guide the teams in creating a rough outline or storyboard for their presentation.
3. Gathering Multimedia Resources (20 minutes):
   - Instruct each team to gather multimedia resources (images, videos, audio clips) related to their chosen theme.
   - Provide guidance on reliable sources and copyright considerations.
   - Encourage students to create their own original content if possible.
4. Creating the Multimedia Presentation (40 minutes):
   - Instruct the teams to use presentation software to create their multimedia presentations.
   - Guide them in integrating their gathered resources, text, and visuals effectively.
   - Encourage creativity in the design and layout of the presentation.

- Presentation Rehearsal and Refinement (20 minutes):
  - Allow each team time to rehearse their presentations and make any necessary refinements.
  - Encourage peer feedback and provide guidance on effective presentation techniques.
  - Support teams in addressing any technical issues or challenges they encounter.
- Presentation and Reflection (15 minutes):
  - Give each team an opportunity to present their multimedia presentation to the class.
  - Instruct them to explain their chosen theme, the STEAM elements integrated, and their creative approach.
  - Facilitate a class discussion where students can provide feedback and ask questions about the different presentations.
- Reflection and Closure (10 minutes):
  - Ask students to reflect on the creative project experience and the connections they made between STEAM and creativity.
  - Discuss the importance of effective communication, multimedia skills, and collaboration in conveying ideas.
  - Summarize the key takeaways from the lesson and highlight the value of creativity in expressing and sharing STEAM-related concepts.

Resources:
- <u>Kids App Maker</u>
- <u>MIT App Inventor</u>
- <u>Infinite Arcade</u> gaming app ($)

Design Challenge Task Cards
Copy and cut out before distributing to students

Astronaut exercise in space – how can we keep our astronauts in tip-top shape? Come up with new space exercises, games, and activities.

Design and create your own app!

AR/VR – augmented and virtual reality! What's the difference? What can we do with these technologies?

Wheeeeeeeeee, PVC! PVC pipes can be used to create many things. Come up with a new tool or item using PVC pipes as your main material.

Up in the Air - explore all types of air crafts! Design a new aircraft using any materials provided.

Math All Around Us – A look at how math affects us in every part of our lives, from math in nature to money, to math in music, and in games we love to play. Explore how math affects the world around us and explain your most interesting findings.

All About Animals! Look into animal adaptations and prosthetics. Come up with a new design of adaptation or prosthetics for any animal.

Board/ Card Game Design – Go old school and create your own board game or card game.

Be an Eco-Innovator! Look at how we can better our planet. Think about renewable energy, sustainable materials, and responsible waste management. Come up with a solution to help preserve our planet.

Scale it up! Pick your favorite logo, store, or candy wrapper and scale up the size. Show the class how you did it.

Week 5

Computer Science and Data Science

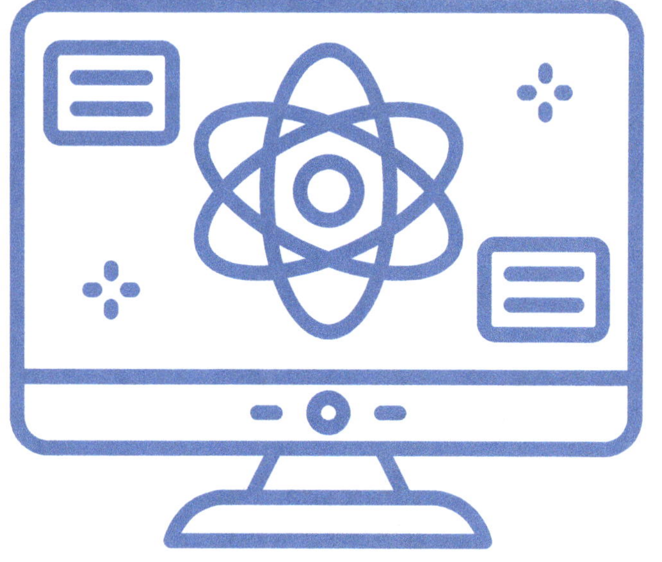

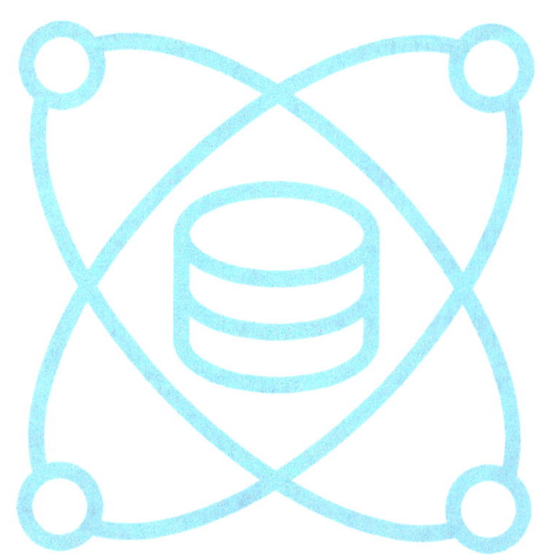

Introduction to Computer Science Concepts

Objective: Introduce students to fundamental computer science concepts, including programming and web development.

Materials:
- Computers or laptops with internet access
- Coding platforms or software (e.g., Scratch, Code.org, HTML editors)
- Handouts with coding exercises or tutorials

Procedure:
1. Introduction (10 minutes):
   o Begin the lesson by explaining the importance of computer science in today's digital world.
   o Discuss the broad range of applications and career opportunities in computer science.
2. Programming Concepts (20 minutes):
   o Introduce the concept of programming and its role in creating software and applications.
   o Explain key programming concepts such as algorithms, variables, loops, and conditionals.
   o Demonstrate examples of simple programs and explain how they work.
3. Hands-on Coding Activity (40 minutes):
   o Provide students with coding platforms or software suitable for beginners (e.g., Scratch, Code.org).
   o Guide them through hands-on coding exercises or tutorials to create simple programs.
   o Encourage experimentation and creativity in their coding projects.
4. Reflection and Discussion (15 minutes):
   o Ask students to reflect on their coding experience and share their observations.
   o Discuss their challenges, problem-solving strategies, and any insights gained.
   o Facilitate a class discussion on the real-world applications of programming.
5. Reflection and Closure (10 minutes):
   o Conclude the lesson by highlighting the relevance of computer science concepts in various industries.
   o Encourage students to explore further coding resources and consider pursuing computer science in their education and careers.

Coding Exercises

Coding is a creative and exciting skill that empowers you to bring your ideas to life. Here are some coding exercises to help you get started and explore the world of programming:

Exercise 1: Drawing Shapes
Write a program that uses basic shapes (such as squares, circles, or triangles) to create a fun and unique design. Experiment with different sizes, colors, and positions to unleash your creativity!

Exercise 2: Guessing Game
Create a program that asks the user to guess a random number between 1 and 100. Provide hints such as "higher" or "lower" to guide the user toward the correct answer. Challenge yourself to make the game more interactive and engaging!

Exercise 3: Mad Libs
Write a program that allows the user to input different words (e.g., nouns, verbs, adjectives) to create a silly story. Use these inputs to fill in the blanks in a pre-defined story template. Get ready for some laughter!

Exercise 4: Calculator
Design a program that functions as a simple calculator. It should allow the user to perform basic mathematical operations such as addition, subtraction, multiplication, and division. Stretch yourself by adding more advanced features like square roots or exponentiation.

Exercise 5: Animated Characters
Create a program that animates a character or object on the screen. You can make it move, change colors, or interact with the user. Let your imagination run wild and bring your creations to life!

Remember, coding is all about practice and persistence. Start with these exercises and gradually challenge yourself with more complex projects. Don't be afraid to experiment, make mistakes, and learn from them. Coding is a journey of discovery and endless possibilities!

Step-by-Step Coding Tutorials

Coding is an exciting skill that allows you to create and solve problems using computer programming. These step-by-step tutorials will help you learn coding concepts and create your own projects. Get ready to dive into the world of coding!

1. Creating a Digital Drawing with Python Turtle:
   - Step 1: Set up your coding environment by installing Python and a code editor like Mu or Thonny.
   - Step 2: Import the turtle module and set up the turtle window.
   - Step 3: Use turtle commands to draw shapes, lines, and patterns.
   - Step 4: Experiment with different colors, pen sizes, and speeds.
   - Step 5: Challenge yourself to create a unique digital drawing using your newfound turtle skills.

2. Building a Maze Game with Scratch:
   - Step 1: Open Scratch and create a new project.
   - Step 2: Design a maze backdrop and add a sprite (character) to navigate through the maze.
   - Step 3: Use Scratch blocks to program the sprite's movements and interactions.
   - Step 4: Add obstacles and collectible items to make the game challenging and engaging.
   - Step 5: Test and debug your game to ensure it works smoothly.
   - Step 6: Share your maze game with friends and challenge them to complete it.

3. Creating an Animated Story with Code.org:
   - Step 1: Visit Code.org and choose the interactive storytelling tutorial.
   - Step 2: Learn about the basics of coding and storytelling concepts.
   - Step 3: Use block-based coding to create characters, backgrounds, and animated scenes.
   - Step 4: Add dialogue, sound effects, and user interaction to enhance your story.
   - Step 5: Publish and share your animated story with others.

4. Designing a Simple Website with HTML and CSS:
   - Step 1: Open a text editor (e.g., Notepad, Sublime Text) to write your code.
   - Step 2: Learn HTML tags to structure your webpage (e.g., headings, paragraphs, images).
   - Step 3: Use CSS to style your webpage with colors, fonts, and layouts.
   - Step 4: Add hyperlinks, buttons, or interactive elements to make your website more engaging.

- Step 5: Preview your webpage in a web browser to see your design come to life.
- Step 6: Share your website with others by hosting it online or presenting it

Remember, coding is about exploring, experimenting, and problem-solving. Don't be afraid to make mistakes and learn from them. Practice regularly, and you'll become a proficient coder in no time. Enjoy your coding journey!

Introduction to Data Science Concepts

Objective: Introduce students to fundamental data science concepts, including data analysis and visualization.

Materials:
- Computers or laptops with internet access
- Data analysis software or tools (e.g., Excel, Google Sheets, Tableau)
- Handouts with data analysis exercises or tutorials

Procedure:

Introduction (10 minutes):
1. Begin the lesson by discussing the importance of data science in extracting insights from data.
   - Explain the role of data analysis and visualization in making informed decisions.
2. Data Analysis Concepts (20 minutes):
   - Introduce the concept of data analysis and its role in examining and interpreting data.
   - Explain key data analysis concepts such as data types, variables, descriptive statistics, and data manipulation.
   - Demonstrate examples of data analysis using software or tools.
3. Hands-on Data Analysis Activity (40 minutes):
   - Provide students with data sets and data analysis software or tools (e.g., Excel, Google Sheets).
   - Guide them through hands-on data analysis exercises or tutorials to analyze and interpret the data.
   - Encourage them to explore different techniques and visualize the data.
4. Reflection and Discussion (15 minutes):
   - Ask students to reflect on their data analysis experience and share their findings.
   - Discuss the challenges they encountered, data patterns discovered, and any insights gained.
   - Facilitate a class discussion on the importance of data analysis in making informed decisions.
5. Reflection and Closure (10 minutes):
   - Conclude the lesson by highlighting the relevance of data science concepts in various fields.
   - Encourage students to further explore data analysis techniques and consider the impact of data in their lives.

Step-by-Step Data Analysis Exercises

Data analysis is an essential skill for making sense of information and drawing meaningful conclusions. These step-by-step exercises will help you practice and apply data analysis techniques to real-world scenarios. Let's dive into the exciting world of data analysis!

Exercise 1: Analyzing Sports Data

- Step 1: Choose a sports dataset (e.g., basketball, soccer, or any other sport you're interested in).
- Step 2: Import the dataset into a spreadsheet software like Microsoft Excel or Google Sheets.
- Step 3: Explore the data by looking at the different variables and their values.
- Step 4: Calculate the average, minimum, and maximum values for a specific variable (e.g., player's scores or team's wins).
- Step 5: Create a bar graph or line graph to visualize the data and identify any patterns or trends.
- Step 6: Write a short summary of your findings and what you can infer from the data analysis.

Exercise 2: Analyzing Population Growth

- Step 1: Find a dataset that includes population data for different countries or cities.
- Step 2: Import the dataset into a spreadsheet software.
- Step 3: Sort the data by population size and identify the countries or cities with the highest and lowest populations.
- Step 4: Calculate the average population and the population growth rate over a specific period.
- Step 5: Create a line graph or bar graph to visualize the population growth over time.
- Step 6: Analyze the data and draw conclusions about the population trends in different regions or countries.

Exercise 3: Analyzing Weather Data

- Step 1: Find a dataset that includes weather data (e.g., temperature, rainfall) for a specific location.
- Step 2: Import the dataset into a spreadsheet software.
- Step 3: Calculate the average temperature or rainfall for different months or seasons.
- Step 4: Create a line graph or bar graph to visualize the temperature or rainfall patterns.
- Step 5: Analyze the data to identify any seasonal trends, such as the wettest or hottest months.
- Step 6: Write a short summary of your findings and discuss the impact of weather patterns on the region.

Remember, data analysis requires careful observation, critical thinking, and drawing conclusions based on evidence. Practice these exercises to sharpen your data analysis skills and apply them to different scenarios. Have fun exploring the world of data analysis!

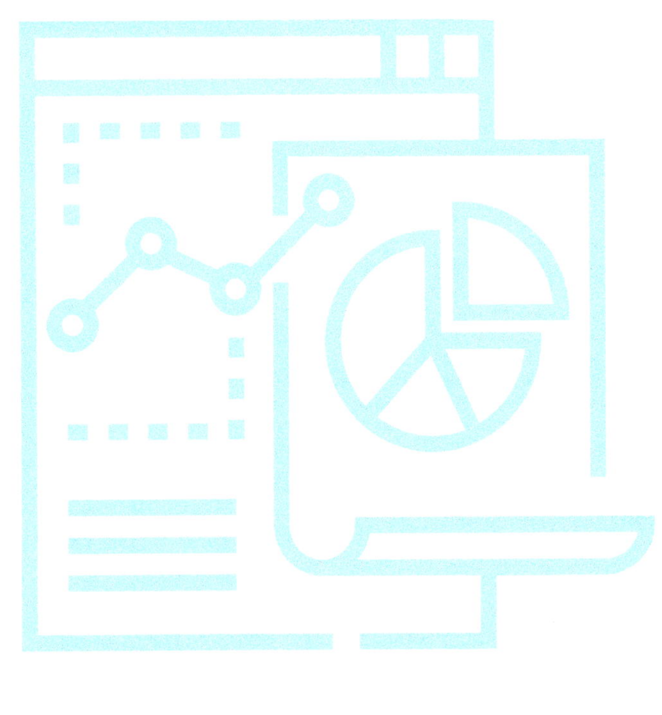

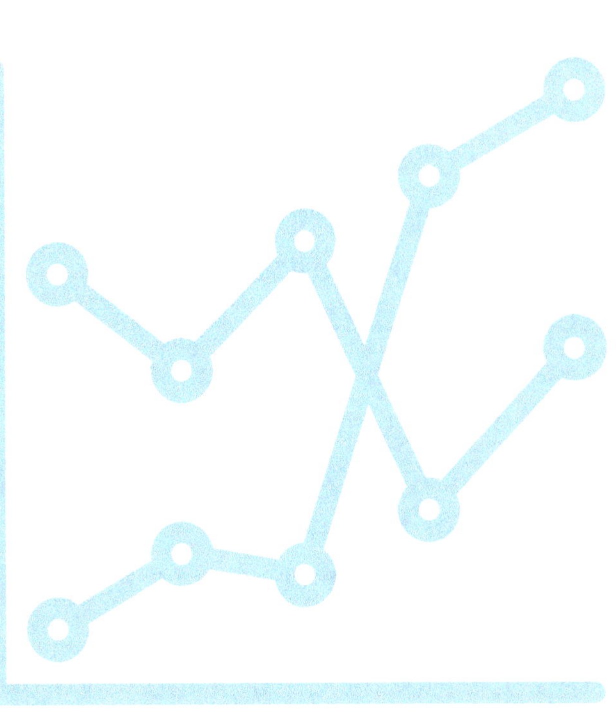

Step-by-Step Data Analysis Tutorials

Data analysis is a valuable skill that helps you make sense of information and draw meaningful conclusions. These step-by-step tutorials will guide you through the process of analyzing data using basic techniques and tools. Let's dive into the exciting world of data analysis!

1. Creating a Bar Graph in Microsoft Excel:
   - Step 1: Open Microsoft Excel and enter your data into a spreadsheet.
   - Step 2: Select the data range and choose the "Insert" tab.
   - Step 3: Click on "Bar Chart" and choose the desired type of bar graph.
   - Step 4: Customize your graph by adding titles, and labels, and changing colors.
   - Step 5: Interpret the bar graph by analyzing the data and drawing conclusions.
2. Analyzing Survey Data with Google Forms and Google Sheets:
   - Step 1: Create a survey using Google Forms to collect responses from participants.
   - Step 2: Export the survey results to Google Sheets.
   - Step 3: Use formulas in Google Sheets to calculate frequencies, averages, and percentages.
   - Step 4: Create charts or graphs to visualize the survey data.
   - Step 5: Analyze the data to identify patterns, trends, or correlations.
3. Exploring Data with Descriptive Statistics in Python:
   - Step 1: Set up your coding environment by installing Python and a code editor like Jupyter Notebook.
   - Step 2: Import the necessary libraries, such as pandas and numpy.
   - Step 3: Load your data into a pandas DataFrame.
   - Step 4: Use descriptive statistics functions (e.g., mean, median, standard deviation) to analyze the data.
   - Step 5: Visualize the data using histograms, box plots, or scatter plots.
   - Step 6: Interpret the results and draw conclusions based on the data analysis.
4. Creating a Line Graph with Data from a Science Experiment:
   - Step 1: Conduct a science experiment and collect data at different time intervals or conditions.
   - Step 2: Organize your data in a table, including the time and corresponding measurements.
   - Step 3: Plot the data points on a graph using a line chart in software like Microsoft Excel or Google Sheets.

- Step 4: Customize the graph by adding labels, and titles, and changing the scales.
- Step 5: Analyze the line graph to understand trends, relationships, or patterns in the data.

Remember, data analysis is not just about crunching numbers; it's about deriving insights and making informed decisions. Practice analyzing different types of data to develop your skills further. Have fun exploring the world of data analysis!

Hands-on Website Development

Objective: Engage students in a hands-on activity to create websites and introduce web development concepts.

Materials:
- Computers or laptops with internet access
- HTML editors or website builders (e.g., Wix, WordPress, Notepad++)
- Handouts with website development resources or tutorials

Procedure:
- Introduction (10 minutes):
  - Begin the lesson by discussing the significance of websites and their role in digital communication.
  - Explain the basics of website development and its relevance in various industries.
- Web Development Concepts (20 minutes):
  - Introduce the basic concepts of web development, including HTML, CSS, and website structure.
  - Explain the role of HTML in defining the structure and content of web pages.
  - Demonstrate examples of HTML tags and their usage.
- Hands-on Website Development Activity (40 minutes):
  - Provide students with HTML editors or website builders (e.g., Wix, WordPress, Notepad++).
  - Guide them through hands-on website development exercises or tutorials to create web pages.
  - Encourage them to experiment with different design elements and customize their websites.
- Reflection and Discussion (15 minutes):
  - Ask students to reflect on their website development experience and share their creations.
  - Discuss the challenges they faced, design choices made, and any insights gained.
  - Facilitate a class discussion on the impact of websites in various contexts.

- Reflection and Closure (10 minutes):
  - Conclude the lesson by highlighting the significance of website development skills in the digital age.
  - Encourage students to explore further web development resources and consider the importance of user-friendly design and accessibility in websites.

Step-by-Step Website Development Resources/Tutorials

Website development is an exciting skill that allows you to create your own web pages and share your ideas with the world. These step-by-step resources will guide you through the process of building a website from scratch. Get ready to unleash your creativity and dive into the world of web development!

- HTML Basics: Creating the Structure of Your Website
    - Step 1: Learn the basics of HTML (Hypertext Markup Language), the foundation of web development.
    - Step 2: Set up a text editor like Notepad or Sublime Text to write your HTML code.
    - Step 3: Start with the basic structure of an HTML document, including the <html>, <head>, and <body> tags.
    - Step 4: Add headings, paragraphs, lists, and links to your webpage using HTML tags.
    - Step 5: Preview your webpage in a web browser to see the structure you've created.
- Styling Your Website with CSS: Adding Colors and Layouts
    - Step 1: Learn CSS (Cascading Style Sheets) to add colors, fonts, and layouts to your web pages.
    - Step 2: Create a separate CSS file and link it to your HTML document using the <link> tag.
    - Step 3: Apply styles to HTML elements using selectors and declarations in your CSS file.
    - Step 4: Customize the appearance of text, backgrounds, borders, and other visual elements.
    - Step 5: Experiment with different CSS properties to enhance the look and feel of your website.
- Adding Interactivity with JavaScript: Making Your Website Dynamic
    - Step 1: Learn the basics of JavaScript, a programming language that adds interactivity to webpages.
    - Step 2: Embed JavaScript code into your HTML document using <script> tags.
    - Step 3: Use JavaScript to create interactive features like buttons, image sliders, or pop-up alerts.
    - Step 4: Write functions to handle user interactions, validate forms, or manipulate webpage elements.

- Step 5: Test your website and ensure that the JavaScript code is functioning as expected.
- Publishing Your Website: Sharing Your Creations with the World
  - Step 1: Choose a web hosting provider to make your website accessible on the internet.
  - Step 2: Register a domain name for your website (e.g., www.yourname.com).
  - Step 3: Upload your HTML, CSS, and JavaScript files to the web hosting server.
  - Step 4: Test your website by visiting the domain name in a web browser.
  - Step 5: Share your website with friends, family, and classmates to showcase your web development skills.

Remember, website development is a creative process, so feel free to experiment and customize your webpages to reflect your personal style. Practice regularly and keep learning new techniques to enhance your website development skills. Enjoy your journey into the exciting world of web development!

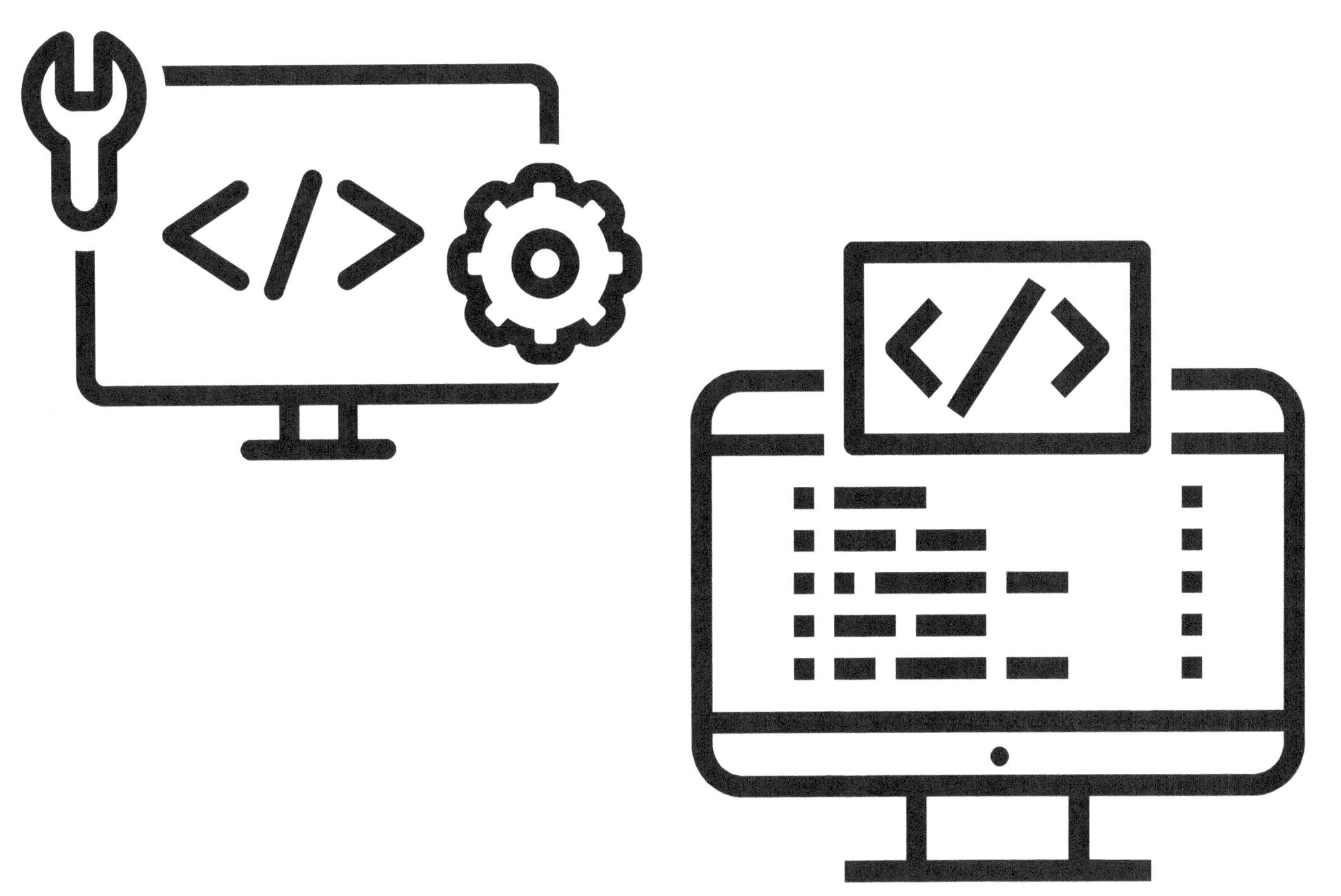

Data Analysis and Visualization

Objective: Engage students in a hands-on activity to analyze and visualize data using data analysis and visualization tools.

Materials:
- Computers or laptops with internet access
- Data analysis and visualization software or tools (e.g., Excel, Google Sheets, Tableau)
- Handouts with data sets for analysis

Procedure:
- Introduction (10 minutes):
    - Begin the lesson by discussing the importance of data analysis and visualization in understanding complex data.
    - Explain how visual representations help in communicating data insights effectively.
- Data Analysis and Visualization Concepts (20 minutes):
    - Review key data analysis and visualization concepts discussed in previous lessons.
    - Explain the importance of choosing appropriate visualization techniques for different types of data.
    - Demonstrate examples of data analysis and visualization using software or tools.
- Hands-on Data Analysis and Visualization Activity (40 minutes):
    - Provide students with data sets and data analysis and visualization software or tools (e.g., Excel, Google Sheets, Tableau).
    - Guide them through hands-on activities to analyze and visualize the data sets.
    - Encourage them to choose appropriate visualization techniques to represent the data effectively.
- Reflection and Discussion (15 minutes):
    - Ask students to reflect on their data analysis and visualization experience and share their findings.
    - Discuss the insights they gained from the visual representations and the effectiveness of different visualization techniques.
    - Facilitate a class discussion on the importance of data analysis and visualization in conveying information.

- Reflection and Closure (10 minutes):
    - Conclude the lesson by highlighting the significance of data analysis and visualization in decision-making processes.
    - Encourage students to further explore data analysis and visualization tools and consider the role of data in various domains.

Data Sets for Analysis

Analyzing data is a valuable skill that helps us understand trends, draw conclusions, and make informed decisions. Here are some interesting data sets to practice your data analysis skills. Have fun exploring these datasets and uncovering insights!

- Weather Data:
  - Description: Daily temperature and rainfall data for a specific location over a year.
  - Source: Local weather stations or online weather databases.
  - Potential Analysis: Analyze seasonal temperature variations, identify the wettest or driest months, or look for patterns in temperature and rainfall.
- Sports Statistics:
  - Description: Player or team performance data for a particular sport (e.g., basketball, soccer).
  - Source: Sports websites, official league websites, or sports publications.
  - Potential Analysis: Compare players' or teams' performance, calculate averages, identify trends, or analyze the impact of specific factors on game outcomes.
- Population Data:
  - Description: Population statistics for different countries or regions.
  - Source: World Bank, United Nations, or government databases.
  - Potential Analysis: Compare population sizes, analyze population growth rates, or identify factors influencing population trends.
- Environmental Data:
  - Description: Data related to the environment, such as pollution levels, wildlife populations, or deforestation rates.
  - Source: Environmental organizations, government agencies, or research institutes.
  - Potential Analysis: Analyze the impact of environmental factors, identify trends, or explore the correlation between human activities and environmental changes.

- Survey Data:
    - Description: Responses collected from surveys on various topics (e.g., hobbies, favorite movies, environmental awareness).
    - Source: Create your own surveys using online platforms like Google Forms or collect data from classmates.
    - Potential Analysis: Calculate frequencies, analyze trends, create charts or graphs, or identify patterns in survey responses.
- Historical Data:
    - Description: Historical events, dates, and relevant information.
    - Source: History textbooks, online historical databases, or museums.
    - Potential Analysis: Analyze timelines, identify significant events, or explore relationships between historical occurrences.

Remember, data analysis is about exploring, asking questions, and drawing conclusions. Use these datasets as a starting point for your analysis, but feel free to add or collect your own data to make it more interesting and relevant. Have fun analyzing the data and uncovering insights!

Week 6

Culminating Project

Identifying Real-World Problems

Objective: Develop students' problem-solving skills by working in teams to identify a real-world problem that can be addressed using their acquired skills and knowledge.

Materials:
- Whiteboard or flip chart
- Sticky notes or index cards
- Markers
- Computers or laptops with internet access

Procedure:
- Introduction (10 minutes):
    o Begin the lesson by discussing the importance of problem-solving skills in real-world scenarios.
    o Explain that students will work in teams to identify a real-world problem and propose a solution using the skills they have acquired.
- Brainstorming (20 minutes):
    o Divide students into teams and provide them with sticky notes or index cards and markers.
    o Instruct each team to brainstorm and write down real-world problems they are passionate about solving.
    o Encourage them to think about issues related to their camp focus and the skills they have developed.
- Problem Selection (15 minutes):
    o Gather the teams' sticky notes or index cards and stick them on a whiteboard or flip chart.
    o Facilitate a group discussion to review and discuss the identified problems.
    o Guide the teams in selecting one problem to focus on for the remainder of the camp.
- Team Planning (30 minutes):
    o Instruct each team to discuss and plan their approach to addressing the chosen problem.
    o Encourage them to consider the skills and knowledge they have acquired during the camp and how they can be applied to solve the problem.
    o Advise teams to outline their solution and identify the steps required for implementation.

- Team Presentations (10 minutes):
    - Allocate a short presentation slot for each team to present their chosen problem and proposed solution to the rest of the camp participants.
    - Encourage teams to provide a brief overview of the problem, their proposed solution, and how their acquired skills and knowledge will be applied.
- Reflection and Closure (10 minutes):
    - Conclude the lesson by facilitating a discussion about the problem-identification process and the importance of using acquired skills for real-world problem-solving.
    - Emphasize the value of teamwork, creativity, and critical thinking in the problem-solving process.

Developing Solutions

Objective: Guide students in developing innovative solutions to real-world problems using the skills and knowledge they have acquired throughout the camp.

Materials:
- Whiteboard or flip chart
- Sticky notes or index cards
- Markers
- Computers or laptops with internet access

Procedure:
- Introduction (10 minutes):
  - Begin the lesson by reviewing the real-world problem each team has selected.
  - Remind students of the importance of developing innovative and effective solutions.
- Solution Brainstorming (20 minutes):
  - Instruct each team to brainstorm potential solutions to their identified problem.
  - Encourage them to think creatively and consider multiple perspectives.
  - Provide sticky notes or index cards and markers for teams to jot down their ideas.
- Solution Selection (15 minutes):
  - Gather the teams' sticky notes or index cards and stick them on a whiteboard or flip chart.
  - Facilitate a group discussion to review and discuss the proposed solutions.
  - Guide the teams in selecting one solution to focus on for the remainder of the camp.
- Solution Development (30 minutes):
  - Instruct each team to further develop their chosen solution.
  - Encourage them to apply the skills and knowledge they have acquired during the camp to refine and enhance their solution.
  - Advise teams to consider the feasibility, impact, and implementation steps of their solution.

- Team Presentations (10 minutes):
    - Allocate a presentation slot for each team to present their developed solution to the rest of the camp participants.
    - Instruct teams to provide a concise overview of their problem, the selected solution, and the rationale behind their approach.
    - Encourage them to highlight how their acquired skills and knowledge have contributed to the development of the solution.
- Reflection and Closure (10 minutes):
    - Conclude the lesson by facilitating a discussion about the solution development process and the importance of innovation and practicality in problem-solving.
    - Emphasize the value of teamwork, adaptability, and perseverance in developing effective solutions.

Final Project Presentations - Part 1

Objective: Provide students with an opportunity to create their final projects and demonstrate their acquired skills, knowledge, and problem-solving abilities through engaging and effective presentations.

Materials:
- Presentation equipment (e.g., projector, computer, speakers)
- Timer or stopwatch
- Computers or laptops with internet access

Procedure:
- Introduction (10 minutes):
  - Begin the lesson by explaining the purpose and importance of final project presentations.
  - Emphasize that it is an opportunity for students to demonstrate their achievements and communicate the value of their projects.
- Presentation Preparation (30 minutes):
  - Remind students of the key components of a successful presentation, such as organization, visual aids, and effective delivery.
  - Review the structure of a presentation, including an introduction, problem description, solution overview, and impact analysis.
  - Provide guidance on creating visually appealing slides, using appropriate graphics or images, and organizing content.
- Practice and Rehearsal (40 minutes):
  - Allocate time for teams to practice their presentations and fine-tune their delivery.
  - Encourage them to rehearse the timing, transitions between slides, and their speaking pace.
  - Provide feedback and guidance to help improve their presentations.

- Presentation Guidelines:
  - Instruct teams to introduce themselves and provide an overview of their project and the problem they aimed to solve.
  - Encourage them to demonstrate their acquired skills and knowledge throughout the presentation.
  - Advise teams to highlight the process they followed, the challenges they faced, and the solutions they developed.
  - Encourage visual aids, such as slides or demonstrations, to enhance the understanding of their projects.
- Reflection and Closure (5 minutes):
  - Conclude the lesson by reflecting on the overall camp experience and the impact of the final project presentations.
  - Encourage students to carry forward the skills, knowledge, and confidence gained through the presentation process.
  - Express gratitude to the students for their active participation and commitment throughout the camp.

Note: It's important to adjust the timings and allocate more or less time for each section based on the number of teams and the complexity of the presentations.

Final Project Presentations - Part 2

Objective: Provide students with an opportunity to showcase their final projects and solutions to a panel of judges or the larger community.

Materials:
- Presentation equipment (e.g., projector, computer, speakers)
- Timer or stopwatch

Procedure:
- Introduction (10 minutes):
  - Begin the lesson by explaining the purpose and format of the final project presentations.
  - Discuss the importance of effective communication and presentation skills.
- Presentation Preparation (30 minutes):
  - Instruct each team to prepare a presentation to showcase their project and solution.
  - Encourage them to organize their content, create visually appealing slides, and practice their delivery.
  - Provide guidance on structuring the presentations, including an introduction, problem description, solution overview, and impact analysis.
- Final Project Presentations (60 minutes):
  - Allocate sufficient time for each team to present their final project to a panel of judges or the larger community.
  - Set up the presentation equipment and ensure it is in working order.
  - Encourage teams to deliver engaging presentations, highlighting their problem-solving approach, solution development process, and the application of their acquired skills and knowledge.
- Q&A and Feedback (15 minutes per team):
  - Allocate time for the panel of judges or the larger community to ask questions and provide feedback after each presentation.
  - Encourage constructive feedback and suggestions for improvement.

- Reflection and Closure (10 minutes):
    - Conclude the lesson by reflecting on the final project presentations and the overall camp experience.
    - Facilitate a discussion about the learning outcomes, challenges faced, and accomplishments achieved by the teams.
    - Emphasize the importance of effective communication and teamwork in showcasing and presenting their projects.

Note: If a panel of judges is not available, the presentations can be conducted in front of the larger camp community, including fellow students, camp staff, and invited guests.

Vocabulary

Science: The systematic study of the natural world, including the observation, experimentation, and analysis of phenomena to gain knowledge and understanding.

Technology: The application of scientific knowledge and tools to create, design, and develop practical solutions or devices that address human needs or improve existing processes.

Engineering: The application of scientific and mathematical principles to design and create structures, systems, machines, and processes that solve problems and meet specific goals.

Arts: Creative expressions of human imagination, skill, and imagination that evoke emotional responses and communicate ideas through various mediums such as visual arts, performing arts, and music.

Mathematics: The study of numbers, shapes, patterns, and quantities, as well as the relationships and properties that govern them, enabling logical reasoning and problem-solving.

Design Thinking: A problem-solving approach that involves empathizing with users, defining problems, ideating potential solutions, prototyping and testing, and iterating to create innovative and human-centered designs.

Coding: The process of writing instructions or commands in a programming language to create software, websites, apps, or control machines.

Robotics: The design, construction, programming, and operation of robots, which are automated machines that can perform tasks autonomously or with human guidance.

Data Science: The interdisciplinary field that involves extracting insights and knowledge from large datasets through methods such as data analysis, visualization, and machine learning.

Experiment: A scientific procedure undertaken to make observations, test hypotheses, and gather data to validate or refute a scientific claim.

Vocabulary

Circuit: A closed loop or path through which electric current flows, typically consisting of conductive wires and various components such as resistors, capacitors, and transistors.

Geometry: The branch of mathematics that deals with the properties, measurements, and relationships of points, lines, angles, shapes, and solids.

Algebra: The branch of mathematics that involves the study of symbols and rules for manipulating these symbols to represent and solve equations and mathematical relationships.

Statistics: The branch of mathematics that deals with the collection, analysis, interpretation, presentation, and organization of numerical data.

Multimedia: The integration of different forms of media, such as text, images, audio, video, and interactive elements, to convey information or create engaging experiences.

Prototype: A preliminary model or version of a design or product, created to test and evaluate its feasibility, functionality, and user experience.

Web Development: The process of designing, creating, and maintaining websites, involving tasks such as coding, scripting, graphic design, and content management.

Analysis: The systematic examination and interpretation of data, information, or materials to gain insights, identify patterns, and draw conclusions.

Empathy: The ability to understand and share the feelings, perspectives, and experiences of others, often used in the design process to develop solutions that meet users' needs.

Innovation: The introduction of new ideas, methods, processes, or products that create significant positive change or address existing challenges in a novel and effective way.

Vocabulary

Physics: The branch of science that studies matter, energy, and their interactions, focusing on principles like motion, forces, electricity, and magnetism.

Chemistry: The branch of science that deals with the composition, properties, and reactions of substances and the changes they undergo.

Biology: The study of living organisms, their structure, function, growth, evolution, and interactions with the environment.

Resources

Online Learning Platforms:
- Khan Academy: Offers free courses in math, science, coding, and more.
- Code.org: Provides interactive coding lessons for students of all ages.
- Scratch: A visual programming language that allows students to create interactive stories, games, and animations.
- Tinkercad: An online platform for 3D design, electronics, and coding projects.

Hands-on Activities and Kits:
- Makey Makey: Enables students to turn everyday objects into touchpads and create their own inventions.
- LittleBits: Offers modular electronic building blocks for creating circuits and inventions.
- Snap Circuits: Allows students to build and experiment with electronic circuits using snap-together components.
- LEGO Mindstorms: Combines LEGO building with coding to create programmable robots.

Science Experiments and Projects:
- Exploratorium Science Snacks: Provides step-by-step guides for hands-on science experiments using everyday materials.
- Science Buddies: Offers a wide range of science project ideas, instructions, and resources.
- NASA STEM Engagement: Provides educational resources, activities, and challenges related to space and science.

Engineering and Design Resources:
- Engineering Design Challenges by TeachEngineering: Offers a collection of engineering projects and lesson plans for various grade levels.
- DIY.org: Provides a platform for kids to explore different skills, including engineering and design, through challenges and projects.
- Instructables: Offers step-by-step instructions for various DIY projects and crafts.

Resources

<u>Art and Creativity Tools:</u>
- Canva: Allows students to create graphics, posters, and presentations.
- Tinkercad: Enables students to design 3D models and creations.
- Art for Kids Hub: Provides step-by-step drawing tutorials and art projects for kids.

<u>Robotics and Coding Resources:</u>
- VEX Robotics: Offers robotics kits and curriculum for students to learn and build robots.
- EV3Lessons: Provides tutorials and resources for LEGO Mindstorms EV3 programming.
- CS First by Google: Offers coding curriculum and activities for beginners.

<u>STEM Challenges and Competitions:</u>
- Future Problem-Solving Program International: Engages students in creative problem-solving and critical thinking.
- FIRST LEGO League: Combines robotics and innovation challenges for students to solve real-world problems.
- Science Olympiad: Organizes science competitions with various events covering different STEM disciplines.

Remember to adapt these resources based on the specific age group and interests of your camp participants. You can mix and match these resources to create a well-rounded STEAM summer camp experience.

Websites

Website: https://www.sciencebuddies.org/
Science Buddies - Provides a wide range of science project ideas, instructions, and resources for students.

Website: https://code.org/
Code.org - Offers interactive coding lessons and activities for students of all ages.

Website: https://www.exploratorium.edu/
Exploratorium - Offers online exhibits, science activities, and experiments for hands-on learning.

Website: https://www.nasa.gov/stem
NASA STEM Engagement - Provides educational resources, activities, and challenges related to space and science.

Website: https://www.pbslearningmedia.org/
PBS LearningMedia - Offers free educational videos, lesson plans, and interactive activities on various STEAM topics.

Website: https://scratch.mit.edu/
Scratch - A visual programming language that allows students to create interactive stories, games, and animations.

Website: https://www.khanacademy.org/
Khan Academy - Provides free courses and tutorials in math, science, coding, and more.

Website: https://www.tinkercad.com/
Tinkercad - An online platform for 3D design, electronics, and coding projects.

Website: https://www.instructables.com/
Instructables - Offers step-by-step instructions for various DIY projects and crafts.

Website: https://kids.nationalgeographic.com/
National Geographic Kids - Provides educational articles, videos, and games on various STEAM topics.

Websites

Website: https://learninglab.si.edu/
Smithsonian Learning Lab - Offers digital resources, exhibits, and interactive activities from the Smithsonian Institution.

Website: https://mysteryscience.com/
Mystery Science - Provides engaging science lessons and activities with hands-on investigations.

Website: https://blockly.games/
Blockly Games - Offers a series of programming challenges for beginners to learn coding concepts.

Website: https://www.nasa.gov/kidsclub/index.html
NASA Kids' Club - Provides educational games, videos, and activities related to space and NASA missions.

Website: https://www.egfi-k12.org/
Engineering Go For It (eGFI) - Offers engineering activities, articles, and resources for students.

Website: https://www.steampoweredfamily.com/
STEAM Powered Family - Provides STEAM project ideas, hands-on activities, and resources for parents, teachers, and students interested in STEAM education.

Website: https://www.eie.org/
Engineering is Elementary - Provides engineering-focused curriculum materials, professional development resources, and hands-on activities for K-12 educators.